BRUNO MINARDI

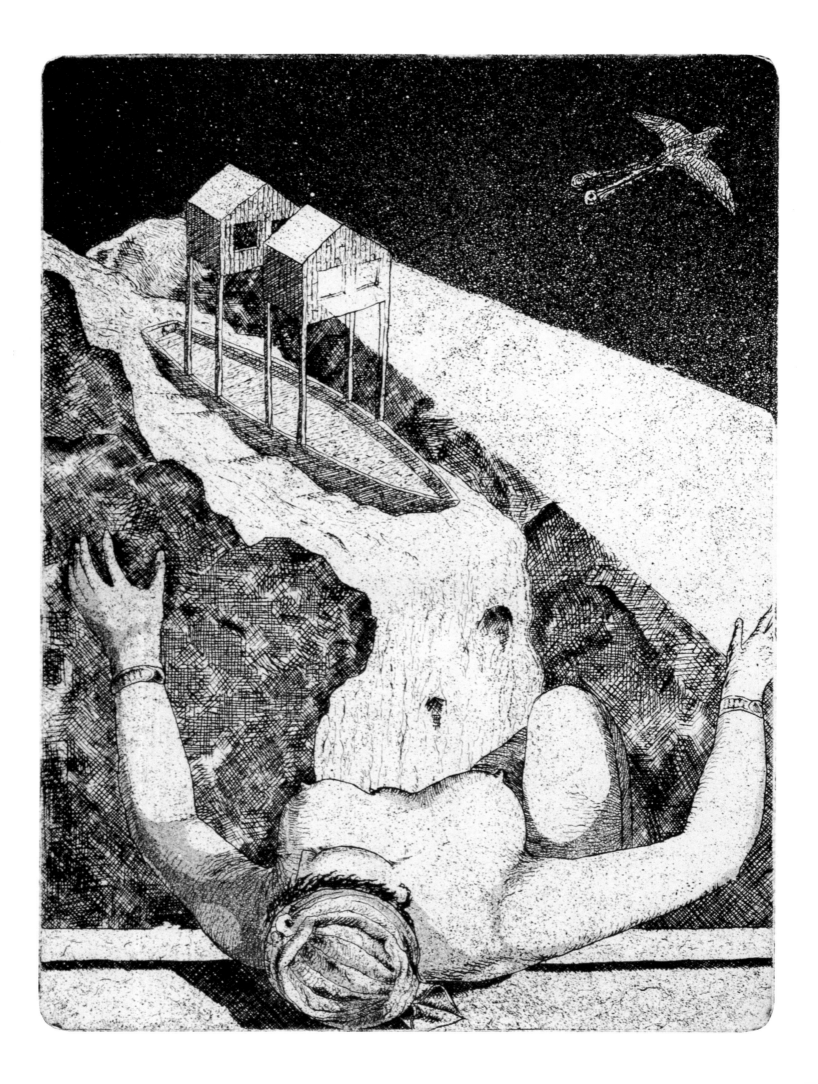

Architectural Monographs No 51

BRUNO MINARDI

A.D. ACADEMY EDITIONS

ACKNOWLEDGEMENTS

This book is dedicated to my wife Claudia and my son Camillo.
My special thanks go to Ettore Brunetti who has gathered together the material for this book, and without whose encouragement it would never have been written, and to Fabrizio Da Col for the final compilation. I would also like to thank Mario and Andrea Bettella at Artmedia who have worked closely with me, conceiving the design and transforming the material into the finished form of the monograph, and Rachel Bean for her work on the text.

Photographic and Picture Credits
All photographs are by Marco Buzzoni unless stated otherwise; every effort has been made to locate sources and to credit material but in the very few cases where this has not been possible our apologies are extended: p9 19th-century German lithograph, *Arctic Fauna*, Bruno Minardi's collection; p19 (below right) Jacopo de Barbari, *Venice Arsenale*, 16th-century engraving and nineteenth-century map both reproduced courtesy of the Museo Correr, Venice; p26 (below centre) Giorgio de Chirico, *Piazza d'Italia*, 1913, private collection; p26 (below right) Giuseppe Pistocchi, project for a theatre for Milan, 1809, reproduced courtesy of the Biblioteca Comunale di Faenza; p34 (below left) Place Royal, Paris, 17th century, from the Plan de Turgot, Bruno Minardi's collection; p34 (below centre) Giorgio de Chirico, *La Torre Rossa*, 1913 reproduced courtesy of the Peggy Guggenheim Foundation, Venice; p37 (below right) Giorgio de Chirico, *La Nostalgia dell'infinito*, 1914, detail, reproduced courtesy of the Museum of Modern Art, New York; p40 (below right) detail of painting showing the old Rialto bridge from Vittore Carpaccio, *The Legend of the Cross*, 1495, reproduced courtesy of the Museo dell' Accademia, Venice; p74 (right above) Giovanni Fantozzi, view of the River Arno, 18th century, Bruno Minardi's collection; p74 (right, centre) Giotto, *Expelling the Devils from Arezzo*, 14th century, detail, Chiesa Superiore di S Francesco, Assisi; p96 (below right) Antonio Canaletto, view of the Grand Canal, 18th century, detail, reproduced courtesy of the Museo Correr, Venice; p102 (centre) historical view of Dubrovnik, 1667, reproduced courtesy of Museo Civico, Dubrovnik; p122 (below, right) *Paesaggio Urbano*, Mario Sironi, 1943, reproduced courtesy of The Jucker Collection, Milan.

Front cover: Nostalgia Urbana, *Venice Biennale, detail, acrylic, 500 x 100cm, with Pino Pipoli*
Page 1: Doctor No House, Milan Triennale, 1976, model, with Romano Brandolini
Page 2: Le Bateau Ivre, 1981, engraving, 13 x 18cm
Page 128: The Alpine Theatre, 1980, model

Architectural Monographs No 51
First published in Great Britain in 1997 by
ACADEMY EDITIONS

A division of
JOHN WILEY & SONS
Baffins Lane
Chichester
West Sussex PO19 1UD

ISBN 0 471 97854 X

Other Wiley Editorial Offices
New York • Weinheim • Brisbane • Singapore • Toronto

Distributed to the trade in the United States of America by
NATIONAL BOOK NETWORK, INC
4720 Boston Way, Lanham, Maryland 20706

Printed and bound in Singapore

CONTENTS

FOREWORD

KENNETH FRAMPTON

Like Leon Krier, Giorgio Grassi and many others who have, at various times, been associated with the *Tendenza*, Bruno Minardi is an architect who has been caught, so to speak, in the slipstream of history. There is an unmistakable air of resignation in his work which is mixed with an evocative talent for watercolour rendering, so much so that one is compelled to take his projections at face value; that is to say as oneiric representations rather than as orthographic projections that might some day be realised. There is an undeniable nostalgia in all this; one that is a strategy for living rather than merely a mode of architectural production. Such a stance can perhaps only be successfully adopted today in the European margins, in those still extant interstices of freedom, in which culture is still lying there as a vibrant thing, embedded within the site or inscribed into local history, the now rarely evoked *genius loci* that has disappeared in so many parts of the world.

As in the early work of Aldo Rossi, certain metaphysical icons (one might say archetypes) haunt the panoramas of Minardi's imagination, the generic tower-cum-belvedere, for example, of which he writes:

> the ubiquitous water tower derives from a formal taste for certain nineteenth-century buildings of a philanthropic nature, to become an autonomous structure with a life and form of its own . . . The belvedere has its origins in my fascination for buildings on marshes and sea shores but also, in particular, for certain wooden towers found in the Ravenna pine woods to prevent fires . . . The pylon tower comes from certain watercolours and appears in various projects . . . It is an airy tower realised with metal sections and inspired by high tension pylons, industrial towers and many other structures.

It is at this juncture that the status of Minardi's archetypes becomes unexpectedly ambiguous, for while when taken to extremes they play rather theatrical roles in metaphysical panoramas bordering on the grotesque, they may also, through a subtle change in tone and palette, be read as banal self-effacing instruments with which to deftly enliven an antique monument as in his project for restoring the Gatteo Castle. Here the metaphysical structures are of a more vernacular, part-agrarian, part-industrial origin; an elevated walkway between the remaining ramparts, a lightweight roof equally protective to both visitors and ruins; technical addenda of genre that is sufficiently close to medieval technology in its simplicity as to impart to the act of restoration a temporal uncertainty. Only one piece stands out in this discrete pragmatic proposal as being 'other', namely, the iconic cylindrical tower that stands as a chimeric witness and as a reference to the Paleochristian bell towers that may be found in the surrounding region.

Minardi thinks of himself as a classical architect and yet this identification seems odd when one sets it beside his manifest obsession with the provisional in the history of architecture; with superimposed attic structures of all kinds, with mine-winding gear and water towers, with sluicegate housing and cantilevered addenda, with radio pylons, chimneys, clock towers, piers and the Panoptic iron galleries of the quintessential penitentiary.

Remote cubic houses executed in stone in some timeless moment, long obsolete bastions still zig-zagging their way down to sea, a cluster of bathing huts, a wind tower that recalls the Martello towers of the English coast, all make up his all but imperceptible interventions proposed for the port of San Nicola. This is Minardi at his best, where past, present and future can no longer be clearly distinguished, making up a world which resists consumerism by largely ignoring it. Mutual indifference is a sentiment much prized by Minardi, reflected when he claims, 'my style is to aim for something very far away', a style that is, at the same time, paradoxically linked to Ravenna, the beloved town of his origin. Finally, it should be stressed that Minardi's working method is one that combines the allegorical with a *modus operandi* which is pragmatic and measured, playful and strangely aloof.

INTRODUCTION
PAOLO PORTOGHESI

Although only a few of the truly outstanding works of Italian architecture from the closing years of this century have been built, there exists, nonetheless, a generation of architects – now in their fifties – with a strong cultural identity and a remarkable poetic attitude. Following in the footsteps of their predecessors, and developing the small revolution begun by them, these architects instil their work with a strong sense of autonomy; it is in their *œuvres* that the essence of Italian architecture for the new century can be discerned.

Amongst them, the figure of Bruno Minardi stands out for his self-assurance and his detachment; his indifference to the trend towards violent architectonic forms that has preoccupied some of his contemporaries. Minardi has constructed his poetic world around a few figurative elements with extraordinary candour and determination. This poetic world has its origins in a real place: Ravenna, a city of silence, barely touched by the cold winds of consumer society; but a city not local in the narrow sense of the word, not characterising itself in the mould of an environment encradled by memory. Minardi's architecture is anything but reconciliatory; it establishes a relationship with the places for which it is designed only when the link between the geometrical image and the materials that will define it is established.

However, before this approach phase there is a displacement phase; a stage of removal, when pre-formed elements are inserted, elements that can only aspire to be inhabited by forming a new place. The principal constituents of Minardi's architecture are the cylindrical mass; the serial montage of 'huts' inspired by the cabins on the Adriatic beaches; the overhang supported, as in those wooden structures, by inclined beams; and the addition of parts that seem like add-ons to pre-existing or imaginary buildings – a process that occurs naturally over time in the growth of cities to accommodate the population's changing requirements and expression. Other distinctive characteristics could be added to these, such as the barrel vault with extradoses and Minardi's taste for small volumes projected upwards by slender vertical structures.

All these elements have different references: some Minardi's, some parallel to the vocabularies of Aldo Rossi, Leon Krier, Adolf Loos and Bonadé Bottino. The most characteristic is the cylindrical mass – which Minardi refers to as a distorted image of Theodoric's Mausoleum in Ravenna – with the upper part shrouded by a top sail of steel tubes. Theodoric's Mausoleum was built in the seventh century; its decagonal plan and incomplete state – a pre-existing gallery has been removed – make it an enigmatic and disturbing monument. But it is significant that, in order to place this building at the centre of his poetic world, Minardi modifies it; while rigorously obeying the original structure he bestows a lightness which only our time can allow, freed from hierarchies and constraining conventions.

This cylindrical mass, after its début as a ringed structure in the Crucoli Rural Centre (1972), re-appears as a block in the proposal for a theatre in the centre of Forlì (1975); in the *Gran Bar*, considered for Stamira Square in Ancona (1976-77); and, repeated five times, in his competition entry for Les Halles in Paris (1979). In the eighties, in the competition for the arrangement of the port of Mazara del Vallo, the same theme undergoes a significant variation. After being interpreted as a ring, as a drum and as a volume elevated on stilts, it finally takes the shape of a merry-go-round: a flat cylinder crowned by a conical roof and supported by a sort of umbrella which springs from a central nucleus. The tower houses a restaurant covered in sheet metal, similar to a lighthouse or a ship's turret.

After this novel variation the theme is re-adopted in the form of a cavity in the projects for the San Niccolo Fish Weir, Florence (1986), a hotel in Cortina d'Ampezzo (1989), the Alpine Theatre (1980) and, finally, in a scheme eventually completed: the expansion of a transport company's offices in Ravenna (1987). Here the exquisite detailing, the technological properties, the harmony of the relations between the roofing and the cylindrical body (the temple and the baptistery, but also the head and the body of an insect) make it lamentable that so many projects have remained on paper.

No less significant a motif in Minardi's work is that of the beach cabin, a recurrent theme which certainly relates to Rossi's work, but which is interpreted in a very different way. In fact, whereas Rossi's cabins, often painted in broad stripes, exude a metaphysical nostalgia, Minardi's express the reduction of a noble archetype: that of the temple, in particular the tympanum, which suggests a certain frontality, which, because it is repeated, becomes a chorus. Here it is worth quoting from a passage by Minardi, which reveals his sensibilities and the Mediterranean roots of his cultural experience:

> I remember, during a trip I took years ago, a Roman templet always different and always the same; in some French squares, amongst the lime trees, in other places in France and in Spain, and finally in Evora, in Portugal, where its pillars of local black stone and its capitols of Portuguese pink marble stood out against the whiteness of the Mediterranean houses, amongst the cork trees and the bougainvillaeas.

This confession is the key to his poetic attitude, and is also an acute observation on the 'unity of diversity' which characterises the classical imprint on the Mediterranean landscape, where the identity of places is defined not by the plurality of the languages but by the different dialects with which it is spoken. The archetypes create the unifying tissue, whilst their building materials and their creative adaptation produce their diversity and identity. This process, though still anchored to the objectiveness of the techniques and the constructions, doesn't deprive the individual expression of space; on the contrary, it makes it possible and natural, protecting it from sterile conflict with the environment and the equally sterile imitation.

One might ask the reasons for Minardi's predilection for certain elements and for their different incarnations; his answer is supplied in the form of a poetic declaration: the 'always identical idea', reminiscent of Mallarmé, Mondrian and, in particular, Morandi, painter of interminable bottles. He writes:

> The repeated idea, seemly identical, is always slightly different, it assumes, in the inclination of a roof, in the dimension of a window, in the construction materials, its own indissoluble localisation which does not express itself through the whims and artificiality of man, but through the great rules of nature . . .
>
> . . . Seasons and weather finally fix the architecture to the landscape: rain, sun, snow, silent and inescapable fogs all become an integral part of my projects.

But how compatible are these simple and alarming forms (which have prompted Bruno Zevi – with reference to the project for Stamira Square in Ancona – to talk about 'hallucinating rigour') with a research which refutes at all costs the originality and the novelty of what is modern? The restaurant at the canal port in Mazara del Vallo does not encourage consonance with the environment nor does it try to induce in the observer that sense of familiarity with the timeless. On the contrary, it imposes itself; it aims to influence its surroundings with a quality that comes from afar, like a message in a bottle. It doesn't expect the surroundings to change, to conform to a rule; the project is a fragment, and so it must remain despite the incomplete state to which we are condemned by a society that is both anarchic and authoritarian at the same time. For this reason the architectural object must be original because it is the originator (as Gaudí said, 'Originalidad es volver a las origines'). It is linked to an archetype and therefore to nature, from which all archetypes derive, and it seems only right that he who rediscovered it and made it grow miraculously from caterpillar to butterfly shouldn't tire of using, perfecting and articulating it, thereby demonstrating its strength and persuasive force. One can use the metaphor of acting and say that Minardi adapts the cylindrical machine to interpret the most diverse roles – the tragic, dramatic and comical – without ever revealing his true personality.

The latest incarnation of the ubiquitous cylindrical mass, the Alpine Theatre, confirms this hypothesis: the actor reveals himself, theatre within theatre; a theatre without stage because the shell is the theatre and the play at the same time. Ascending the narrow spiral staircase, one passes through a pyramid to discover at the end the form of a theatre, a series of concentric circles drawing the spectator's gaze towards the open vortex down below. Calvino, Borges, Jonesco and Beckett could be acted in this theatre.

As in a film by Marcel Carné, it is a merry-go-round spinning joy and pain, the banal and the sublime; it blends them; it amalgamates them. This is the union of a merry-go-round and a neo-classical theatre (specifically, Giuseppe Pistocchi's project for Milan, 1809). The carousel is so everyday that is colloquially known as *calcinculo* (kick-up-the-arse). But is the merry-go-round really so vulgar and ugly? Isn't this useless machine one of the few high notes in the greyness of the squalid suburban environment – in the midst of green fields which are littered by the piles of refuse that plague the environs of the city?

What Minardi's architecture is trying to tell us is that the banal and the sublime can travel together, can even merge in a metamorphosis. Wasn't this, after all, Rimbaud's discovery? Perhaps this is what Minardi intends when, by refusing the worn out 'post-modernist' label, he declares himself a 'premodernist'; he is on the side of those who don't claim to design the world or preach palingenesis but who want to *changer la vie*, to render the world a better place in which to live.

Arctic Fauna, *19th-century*
German lithograph

THE ETERNAL RETURN OF THE SAME

BRUNO MINARDI

The profound rapport I have with the traditional is evident in my first project, the Manetti House, which was designed when I was still a student. This rapport is not to be understood as imitation but rather as an approach in which continuity is maintained by means of analogy. Above all, the house initiated an understanding of 'architecture without architects', in which design is achieved by absorbing a limited number of formal archetypes from the world around us, to produce a formal empathy which is perhaps innate as much as it is inexplicable. Conceived in 1969, the Manetti House provided the basis from which certain architectural elements have been developed and redeveloped. These elements may often be technical features which have practical rather than representational purposes, but which in their simplicity and repetitiveness acquire the nature of real 'types' to which one may refer.

The first of these elements is the bell tower with its simple, elongated forms (the first bell tower was built in tenth-century Ravenna). Then there is the Venice Arsenale: a great building that rises from the water, repeating its great workshops with their lean-to roofs placed at right-angles to the main facade. The image of the Arsenale, which I first discovered when I was at university, has become a recurring obsession in my formal world; it becomes an original and useful way to occupy, subdivide and transform space in architecture by means of repeated elements of construction.

Another great love was kindled by industrial scenes, which identify, through simple repetition, a catalogue of essential elements characterised by latent classicism: iron sheds, roofs, silos, tanks, and the large-scale port equipment of the dockyard. I consider industrial archaeology to be the only innovative architecture of this century. Being more inclined towards an understanding of architecture as a fragmentary rather than a continuous addition, I have adopted similar elements in my formal repertoire which reappear in slightly modified form from one project to another, such as the great cylindrical vessel. This architecture, which has its origins in strong formal suggestions from buildings which often do not constitute 'architecture', finds a home by merging into the heritage of the historic city: its squares, baptisteries, places of worships, 'cloned' houses and so on.

For me, the roots of architecture are always in its location. Invariably, it is born and grows out of something already present. In this sense, architecture is always an addition.

I am not influenced specifically by other architects but by the buildings around us, and by painters such as Giotto, Ambrogio Lorenzetti, Vittore Carpaccio and Giorgio de Chirico. Finally, if the paradox is permissible, I identify myself as a naturalist rather than a rationalist, making choices in design and materials which are linked more closely to the factors of nature (latitude, weather, local building tradition) than those which are purely intellectual.

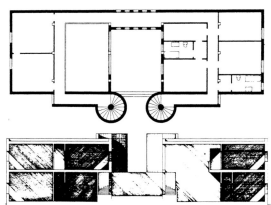

MANETTI HOUSE

RAVENNA, 1969-70

Minardi produced this design while still a student. The house is located in a suburban development not far from Ravenna, where most of the other buildings are one-family villas. Here Minardi had to overcome a number of difficulties which included the lack of a well-defined urban setting to refer to (with the exception of that established by current building regulations); the lack of formal values in the vicinity; and the lack of space available for a garden due to the lot dimensions.

In response, the building was developed from the inside and was organised, formally and functionally, around a central courtyard. The courtyard provides a typological space offering a range of possible design solutions, each of which can only be developed by following a determined and definite plan.

Its individual components were defined by using simple geometric volumes in an additive process that makes the clarity of the whole building evident. Thus the spaces in the villa have been conceived as 'landmarks' for the various functions (or rooms) and have been

determined so as not to impinge on the owners' freedom when designating areas for them – though there are provisional divisions.

The distinctive forms of the towers draw on the local tradition of *campanile* and Ravenna's Roman gateway.

With C Giuseppe, C Baldisserri, G Grossi

ABOVE: **Rear facade (seated on the left is Bruno Minardi and on the right, Claudio Baldisserri);** *BELOW, L TO R:* **San Vitale, Ravenna, 6th century; plan and section; Santa Agata, Ravenna, 11th century**

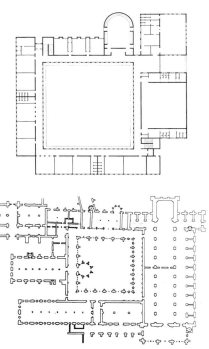

SCHOOL IN MARINA DI RAVENNA

RAVENNA, 1971

Located on the outskirts of a seaside resort not far from Ravenna, the school has as its backdrop a large industrial zone of metal towers, enormous petroleum tanks and smoke. Accommodating 375 pupils, it consists of 18 classrooms, a gymnasium, an auditorium, some offices and a refectory.

The school is developed and ordered around a square internal courtyard, on to which all the building's volumes face, either directly or indirectly. A cloister runs round the courtyard affording views of the school

complex, while the specific roles of each of its component parts are indicated by their distinct formal expression. Thus the corridor, transformed into a cloister, maintains its function of connecting internal spaces, while being imbued with meanings that transcend pure utility. Here Minardi drew on the example of the Monastery of Maulbraunn, where a cloister unifies similarly diverse elements.

The classrooms are located in the two two-storeyed wings. The two remaining parts, connected to the rest of the building by two

staircases, contain the refectory, the auditorium, the offices and the gymnasium.

The exterior of the building is painted pale blue; the interiors are whitewashed, and the floors are laid with dark stoneware tiles. A tree has been planted in the courtyard lawn.

With C Giuseppe, C Baldisserri, G Grossi

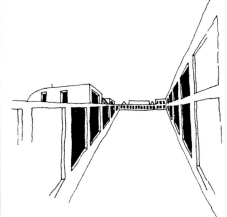

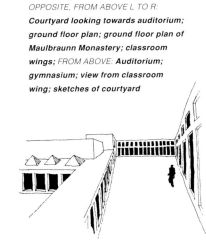

OPPOSITE, FROM ABOVE L TO R:
**Courtyard looking towards auditorium;
ground floor plan; ground floor plan of
Maulbraunn Monastery; classroom
wings;** FROM ABOVE: **Auditorium;
gymnasium; view from classroom
wing; sketches of courtyard**

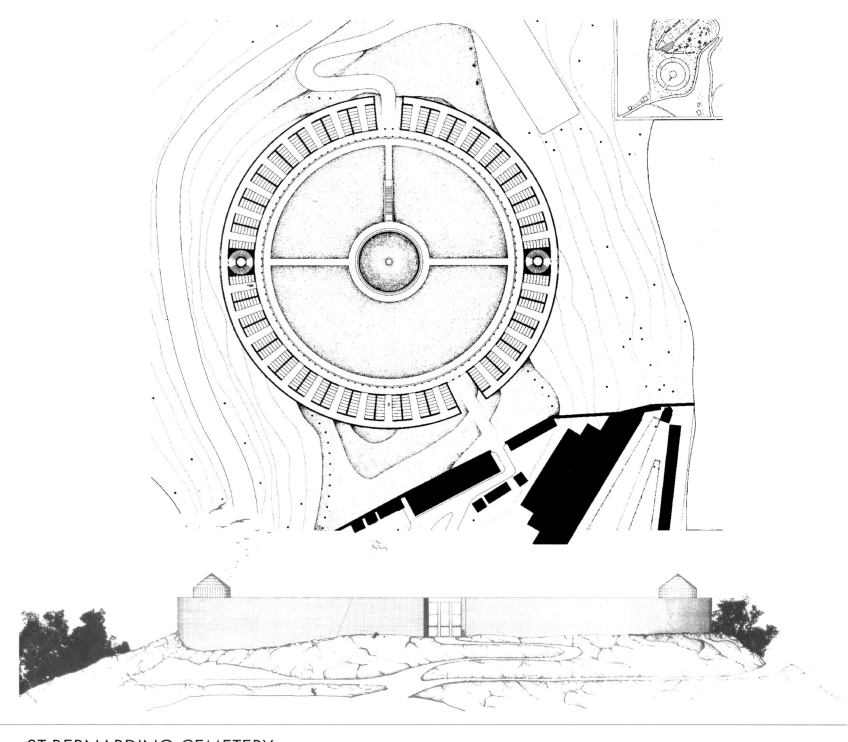

ST BERNARDINO CEMETERY

URBINO, 1982

The area set aside for the competition to expand the cemetery afforded enough space to construct a separate building. This project consists of a single building with a circular courtyard in which there are two kinds of tomb: those on the ground in the centre and those in small chambers in the walls of two of the building's floors.

The focal point of the interior is a memorial to the war dead. This takes the form of an underground domed space, above which two flights of stairs leading to the second floor are accommodated in a cylindrical structure illuminated by a glass cupola. At the top of the stairs the passage through the upper floor affords two beautiful views from openings in the outer walls towards Urbino on one side and the hills on the other. The conical windows give a sense of the internal volume and establish a symbolic rapport with the surroundings.

The forms, such as the white colonnades inside, are reminiscent of Italian cities, of their architecture and piazzas.

Since the surrounding Umbrian landscape is one of undulating hills, the skyline sloping away in every direction, Minardi decided not to rest anything flat on it. Instead, the starting point is a higher plane which reaches down and rests on the ground. In this way the building both transcends and touches the earth. (The drawings for this project are the first to include a kite, a motif that recurs in Minardi's subsequent work.)

With C Baldisserri, G Grossi

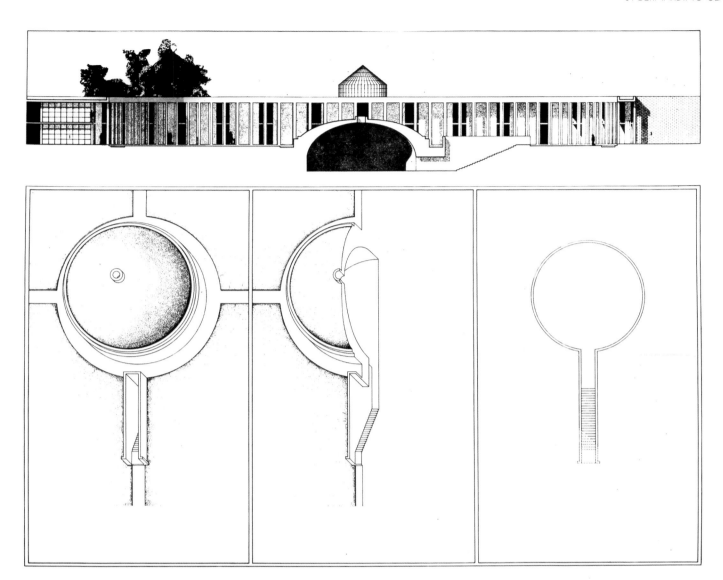

OPPOSITE FROM ABOVE: **Site plan; elevation;** *ABOVE:* **Section and axonometric views;** *LEFT:* **Detail of facade**

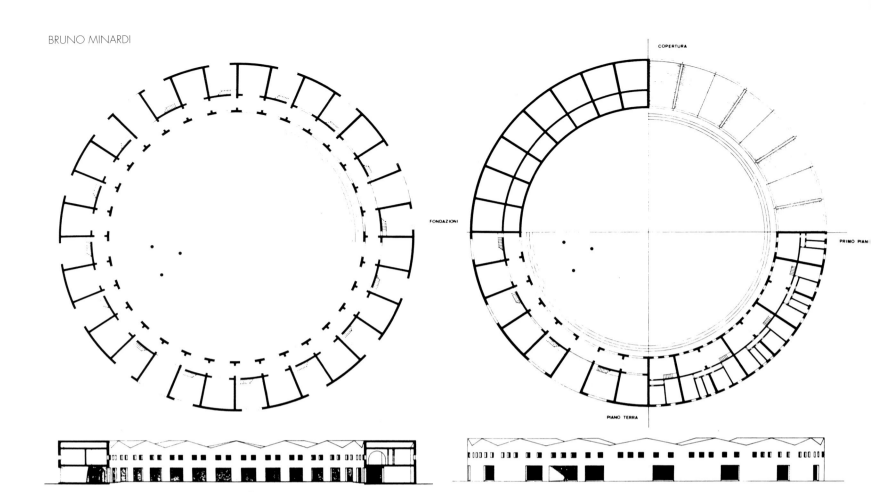

RURAL CENTRE

CRUCOLI, 1972

In designing these buildings for the very large farm of a Calabrian nobleman, Minardi chose to concentrate them in a single group rather than dispersing them over a large area.

He drew not only on his own architectural ideas, but also on the local tradition which has a pronounced identity arising from its feudal culture and economy. He was also reminded of the geometrical rigour of ancient encampments and of the great farm buildings arranged within a single exterior wall with an entrance gate and central courtyard.

However, rather than producing a strictly rural looking building, Minardi aimed for a compromise with the urban. This is apparent in the details.

The resulting design features a ring-shaped building which contains workshops and shops on the ground floor, facing the courtyard with storehouses opening to the outside, and living quarters on the first floor.

The whole was to be constructed in irregular blocks of stone with roof coverings and fittings in metal sheet enamelled pale blue. The front

doors were to be black enamel and the internal portico was to be white stucco.

With C Baldisserri, G Grossi

FROM ABOVE, L TO R: **Ground floor plan; plan showing (clockwise) roof, first floor, ground floor and foundation levels; sections; elevation; market square, Lugo, 18th century; market square, Bagnacavallo, 18th century;** *OPPOSITE, FROM ABOVE L TO R:* **Sketches and studies; axonometric detail; rural building in Crucoli, 18th century; medieval square of Lucca, built on the Roman circus**

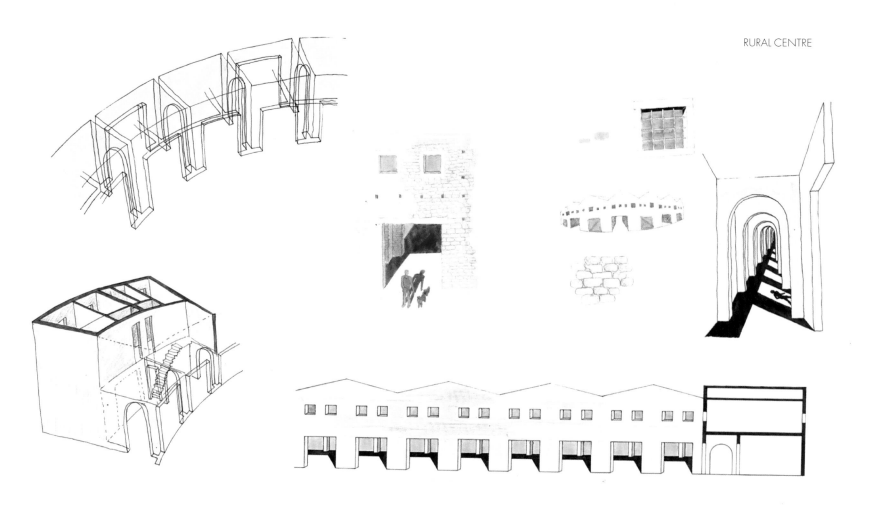

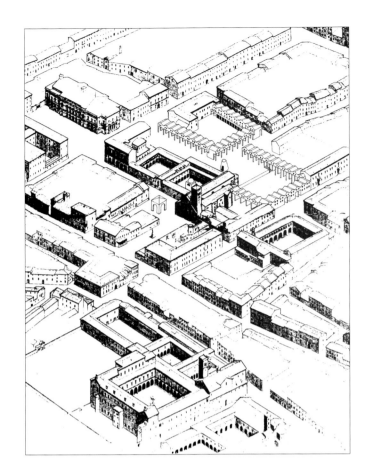
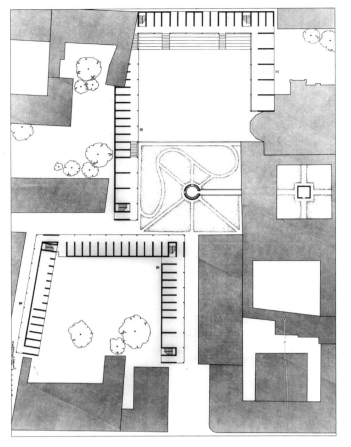

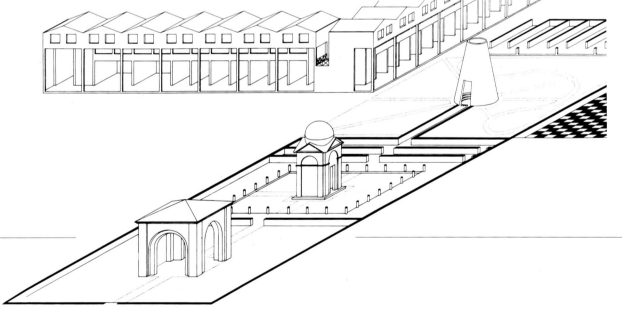

DANTESQUE ZONE
RAVENNA, 1973-74

This project focuses on an area in the centre of Ravenna, bordered by a series of monumental buildings, including the fifth-century church of St Francis, its fifteenth- and sixteenth-century cloisters, and Dante's tomb (eighteenth century). This area is an unresolved part of the town, having yet to find its identity, its forms and functions.

Minardi's plan suggests a courtyard landscaped with trees in order to complete an existing city block, and a two-level square. At the present level of the square a zone is

reserved as a green area with its entrance 'cone' to the 'monumental road' which joins the cloisters to Dante's tomb and the sixteenth-century Braccioforte Chapel; at the old level of St Francis' apse, a zone is reserved as a paved square, accessed from a flight of steps which can also be used as seating for concerts and outdoor meetings.

These spaces are surrounded by buildings with arcades. The serial repetition that characterises these structures is a theme which runs throughout Minardi's work, one that

can be seen to have its origins in the forms of the Venice Arsenale. All the buildings are clad in grey stone, the arcades are white inside, the roofs are enamelled a pale blue.

With C Baldisserri, G Grossi

*FROM ABOVE, L TO R: **View of the existing townscape with Minardi's scheme superimposed; site plan; isometric of the 'monumental road' linking Minardi's conical entrance, Dante's tomb and the Braccioforte Chapel;** OPPOSITE, FROM ABOVE L TO R: **Sections; design variants; Venice Arsenale, 16th-century engraving by Jacopo de Barbari and 19th-century plan***

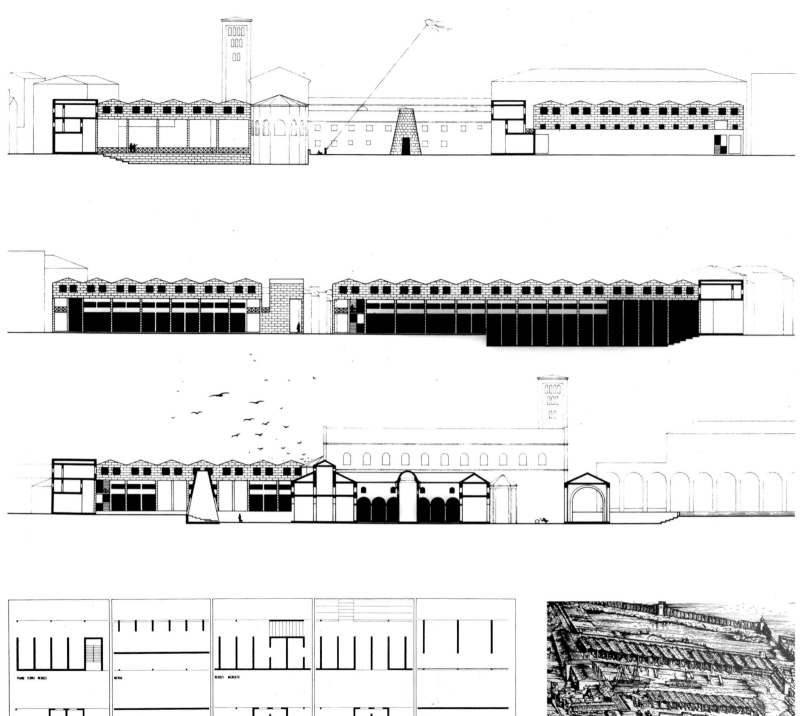

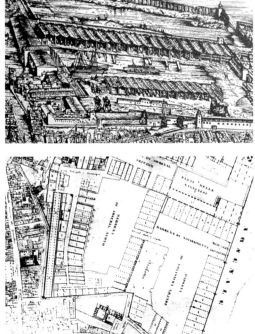

WATERCOLOURS

1975-76

During 1975 and 1976, Minardi painted nine small watercolours. He used this expressive medium in an attempt to prefigure some of the architectonic forms typical of his work. The forms that he created in these paintings have become an integral part of his formal repertory. These watercolours were also inspired by Minardi's desire for architectural nostalgia and mood.

OPPOSITE FROM ABOVE:
Le Bateau Ivre, *9 × 11cm;*
Sometimes, *9 × 11cm; FROM*
ABOVE, L TO R: **The Pagan**
Town, *9 × 11cm;* **The House**
of Doctor No, *11 × 9cm;*
Reisengebirge Night, *11 × 9cm*

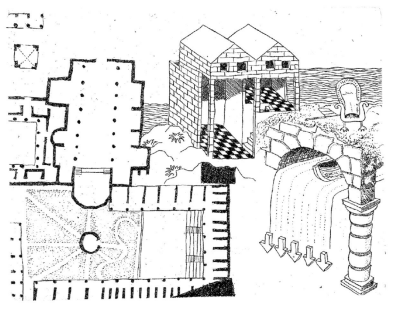

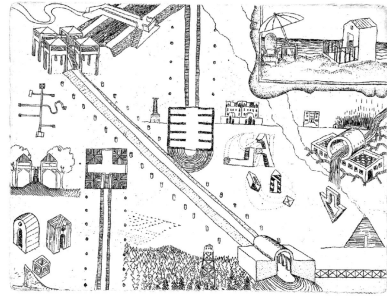

ENGRAVINGS

1974-75

Between 1974 and 1975, Minardi executed ten copperplate engravings which combine creative ideas and a few personal or autobiographical themes, somewhere between design and everyday life.

He has always studied old publications from Piranesi and Rossini's interpretations of Roman ruins to Hogarth's *The Analysis of Beauty*. In addition, he is fascinated by the idea that the process of design might have something in common with herbariums, insect collections and ornithology books: that it is

natural, mechanical and determined, gradually accumulating into a personal catalogue of obsessive ideas.

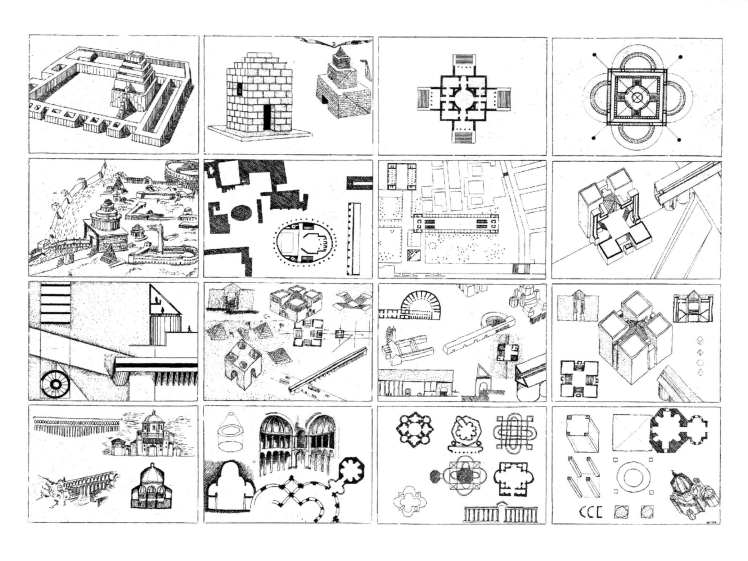

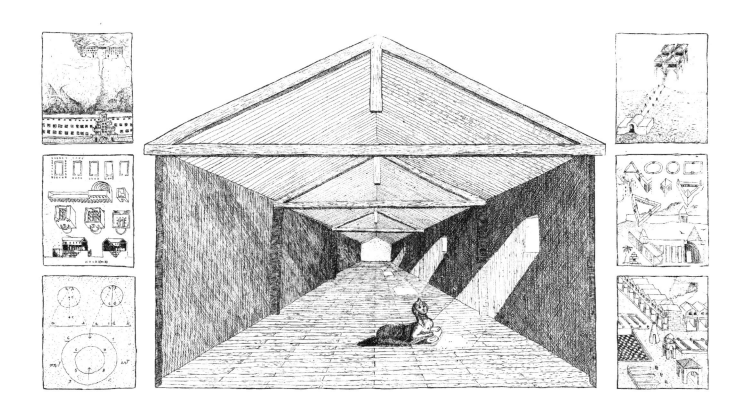

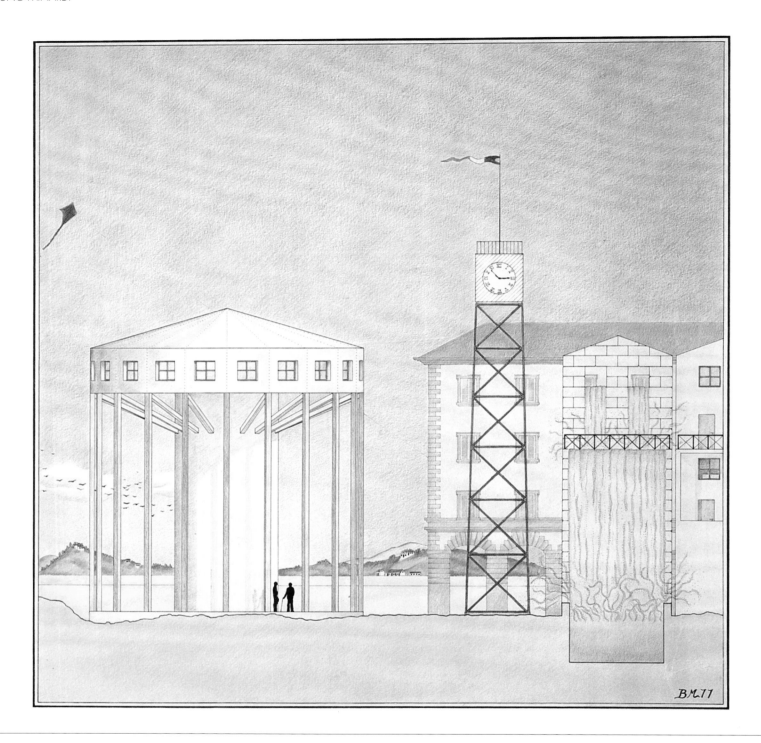

STAMIRA SQUARE

ANCONA, 1976-77

Ancona lies on the Adriatic coast, hemmed in by disparate, recent developments. Stamira Square lies on the edge of the old city but, like the area covered by Minardi's Forlì project, lacks any real sense of cohesion or identity. The isolated architectural elements that do exist are remarkable only in terms of their own history, lacking any cohesion with the rest of the surrounding urban fabric.

The square brought to Minardi's mind distant memories of a funfair, the way it occupies a patch of green snatched from the

city. Thus he viewed it not in terms of a built-up piazza but as an open place in which detached elements work together to create a sense of place.

He proposed a pylon-like watch tower; a monument in the form of a small house with a fountain of cascading water; two residential buildings containing small flats for the young and old; a circular building, inspired by a merry-go-round, with a bar in its top level; and a tank-like building to house markets, exhibitions and other public events.

He notes that his whole approach was permeated by an ill-concealed desire to go back to the abandoned plots, now invaded by weeds, and make them places for children's adventures and lovers' trysts.

With G Grossi

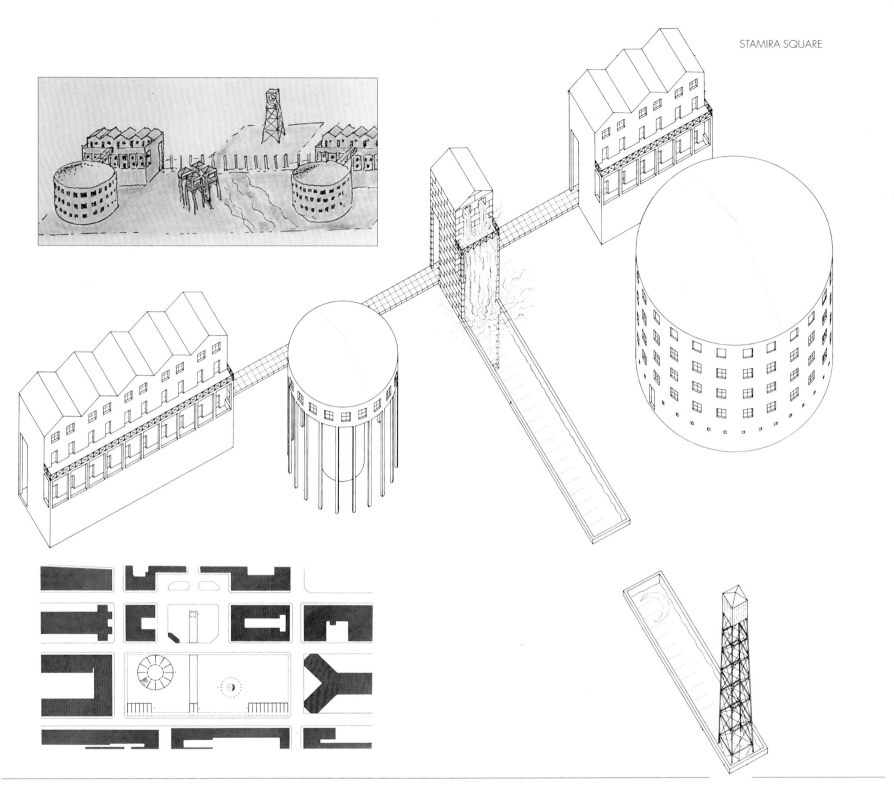

OPPOSITE: *Elements of the project;* FROM ABOVE: *Sketch; axonometric; site plan; elevations*

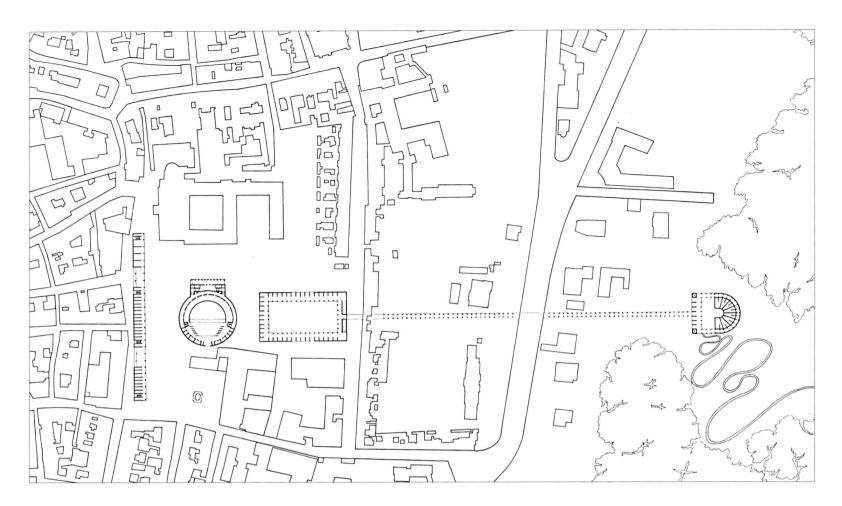

THEATRE IN FORLÌ

FORLÌ, 1975

This project developed from a national competition to site a theatre and a block of council housing in the unresolved, empty space in front of a church. Several factors combined to prevent any real possibility of redefining the city fabric: its incompleteness; its arrangement in an irregular series of spaces; and the incongruous elements that the brief sought to combine.

Thus, Minardi proposed some isolated buildings determined by their own internal rules which later architects could use as the basis for completing the group. These include the theatre and housing block originally specified, a square, an elevated pedestrian route, and an open-air theatre. The last three elements, though not required by the competition brief, were introduced in order to connect the urban centre with a nearby nature park. The built-up, closed square of the scheme reflects local commercial building patterns. The centrally planned theatre is based on Giuseppe Pistocchi's project for a theatre in Milan (1809). The residential block consists of a row of houses linked by a porch and a gallery – exactly like that proposed for the Dantesque zone except for a slight variation: the small clock tower.

With G Grossi

*FROM ABOVE, L TO R: **Site plan; Court of Miracles, Pisa, 11th to 13th century; Giorgio de Chirico, Piazza d'Italia, 1913; Giuseppe Pistocchi, project for a theatre for Milan, 1809;** OPPOSITE, FROM ABOVE L TO R: **Elevation; drawings for council houses; square and walkway; theatre; open-air theatre***

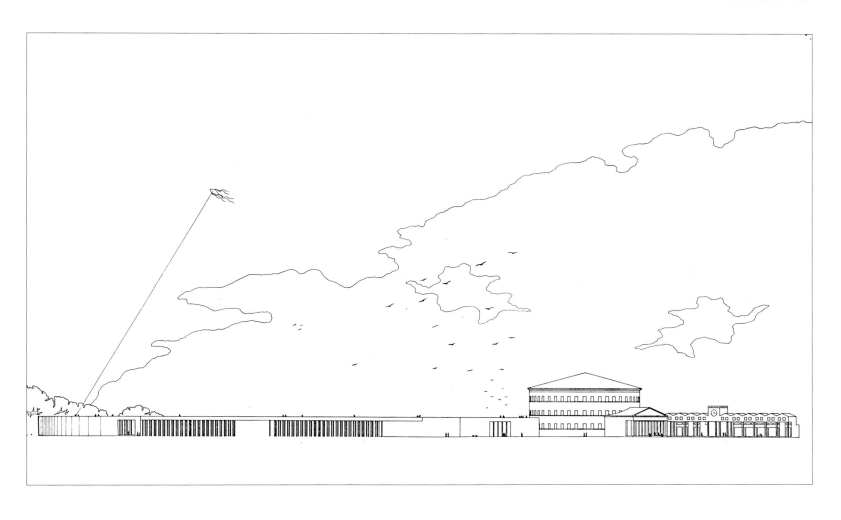

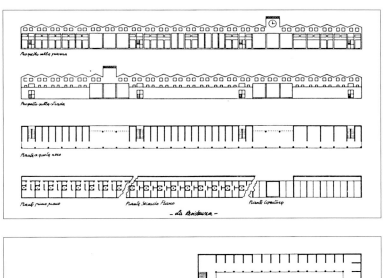

da Pescheria

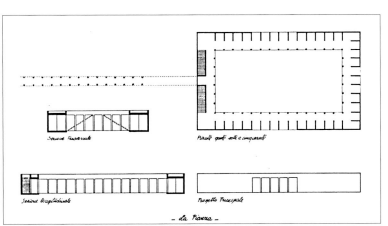

da Piazza

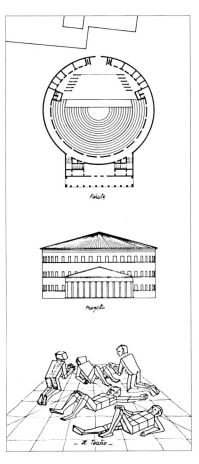

Il Teatro

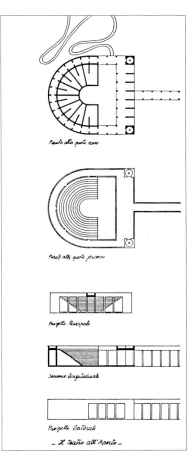

Il Teatro all'Aperto

INCREASING THE HEIGHT OF COUNCIL HOUSES

CESENA, 1977-78

This was the winning project in a competition sponsored by Cesena City Council to double the amount of accommodation provided by two existing parallel buildings along the city ring road. These blocks, totalling 240 metres in length, were constructed in 1923 and follow the simple, rational style of early housing projects; with their clarity of structure, they represent constructive rationalism and progressive urbanity. Due to their position near the road and the garden which has grown up in front of them, they have

contributed to the definition and construction of this part of the city.

All the other competition entries chose to demolish the existing buildings and replace them with towers; Minardi chose to restore and extend them upwards. While such an approach is rare now, it was common in the past when cities grew incrementally. It also provided a fast and easy-to-build solution.

Minardi respected the integrity of the original buildings as much as possible, while affording the new addition character and a

certain degree of autonomy. In order to avoid overburdening the existing foundations, the extension is supported by tall iron portals placed on the outside of the building beneath; these columns create a kind of double arcade around the old building. The use of reinforced concrete sandwich panels, besides ensuring a quicker building time, accentuates the break with the older housing below. The whole consists of two-bedroom apartments for families.

With C Baldisserri, G Grossi, L Dardozzi, M Casadio

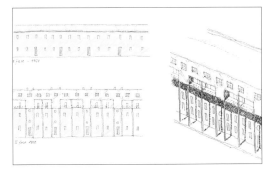

*OPPOSITE: **Drawing of three projects – Cesena houses, Dreher factory and Rafal offices (Ravenna, 1976)**; ABOVE: **Sketches***

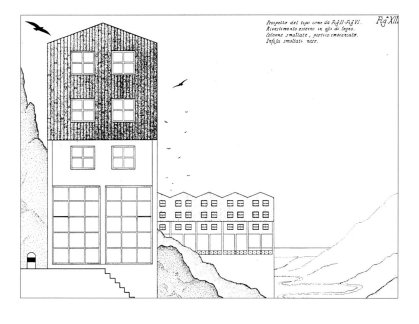 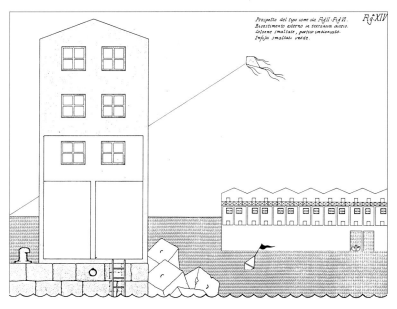

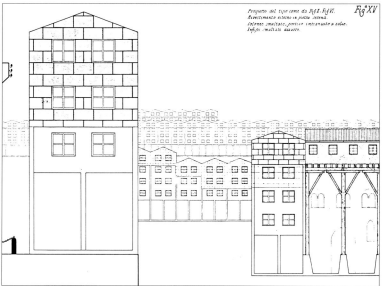 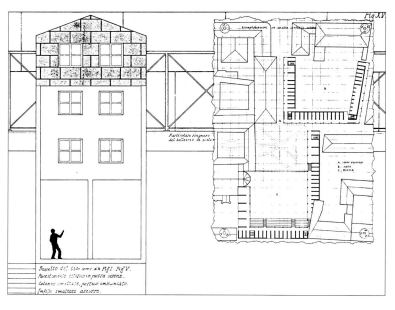

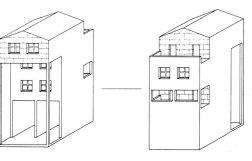 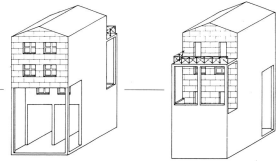

TEMPORARY HOUSES
FOGGIA, 1976

Developed for a competition organised by Foggia Council, this project presents a possible solution to providing temporary housing for council tenants awaiting permanent homes. It is 'architectural' without being based on any specific sociological assumptions. It consists of some possible sections, views and plans of building elements that can be stacked in different ways according to site and circumstance.

The arcade, 5 metres high, signifies the social and collective use of the building.

Behind it are a row of shops, residential services, communal halls and depots. The upper part, set aside for housing, can be adapted to suit the varying needs likely to arise over time. This is possible due to a structural frame that affords a high degree of internal flexibility when forming space; Minardi developed several housing variations to demonstrate the flexibility of the design.

The scheme is characterised by a repetition and layering of elements, the latter drawing on such models as the well-known Malugani

House in Bologna, where an old gothic house was built up with a later structure and portico.

Minardi's project seeks to demonstrate the potential of even the gloomiest place through the considered application of architecture.

Depending on location, the upper part of the building can be clad in grey stone (urban areas), finished in painted plaster (seaside resort), or in treated wood (mountain resorts).

With G Grossi

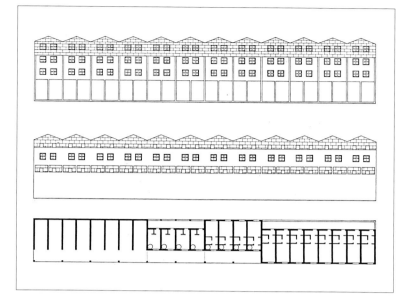

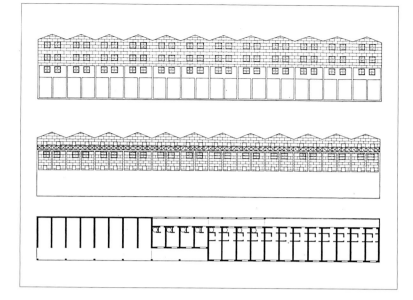

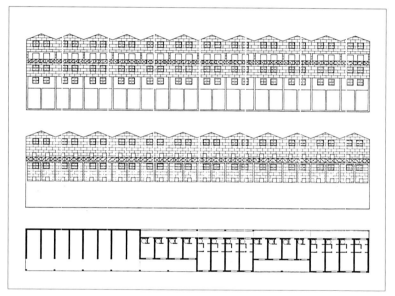

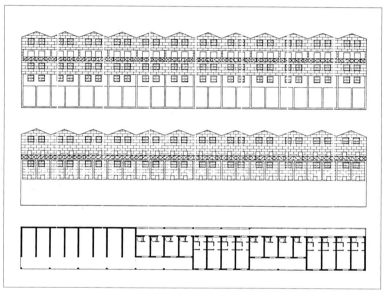

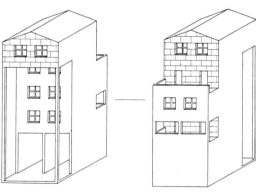

OPPOSITE: *Variations on basic design for different locations – mountain, seaside and urban; axonometrics; FROM ABOVE: Elevations, plans and axonometrics; Bonaiti Malugani House, Bologna, 18th century*

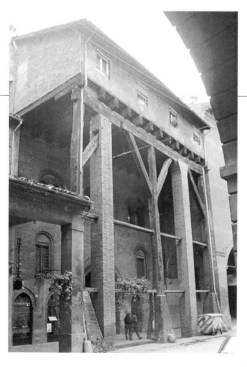

HOUSING IN THE FORMER DREHER BREWERY

VENICE, 1980

The former Dreher Brewery, built at the end of the nineteenth century, stands on the Giudecca Channel. When Minardi converted it to flats, he based his approach on a number of general considerations.

First, the internal floors – which were crumbling and at unusable heights – were to be completely replaced to meet the new requirements of the living quarters and to correspond to the organisation of the existing external windows which could not be changed.

Second, the size of the building made it important to find a way of distributing the apartments. The solution was found in the form of a narrow internal street, covered with a glass roof. This made possible a series of galleries which distribute the various rooms.

Third, the narrow internal alley and various galleries, illuminated by skylights, begin and end on large iron terraces. These are really roof terraces which project outside and are connected by stairwells.

Fourth, the exterior of the building was to be entirely preserved, the only visible sign of the restructuring being a series of glass pyramids on the roof which correspond to the internal gallery.

Finally, the large chimney brings the fire escape right inside the building, connected by two slender footbridges.

With G Gambirasio, G Brusati, G Dorigo, P Gheller

*OPPOSITE: **Plan; sketches***

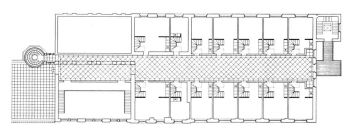

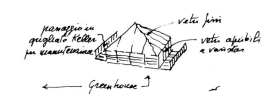

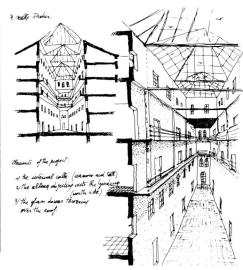

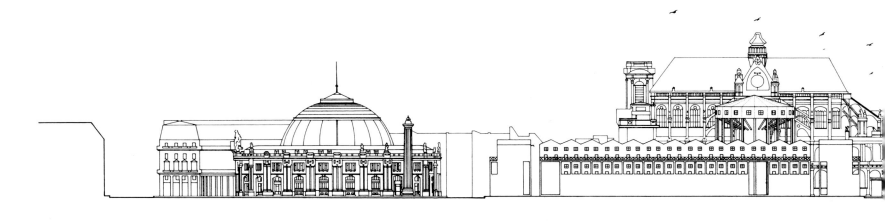

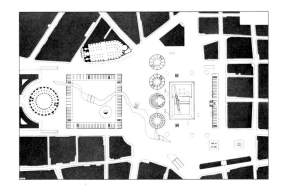

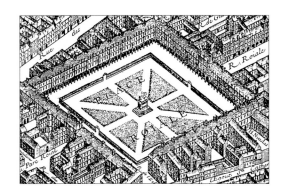

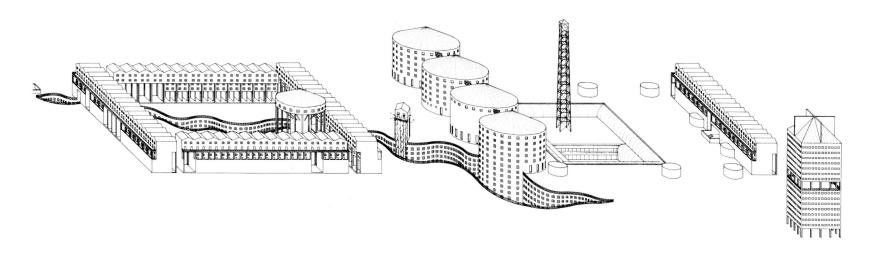

LES HALLES SQUARE

PARIS, 1979

As in Minardi's previous projects for squares, a single, overall solution was not considered desirable for organising the enormous space left in the centre of Paris by the demolition of the old market (Les Halles).

On the huge upper square, left by clearing the space between buildings which were previously obscured from each other, Minardi places a series of structures – 'a kind of metaphysical encampment' – consisting of squares; underground houses; a weather vane tower; a pylon topped by a clock; the ubiquitous drum-shaped buildings which contain a theatre, a museum, a hotel and an old people's home; and, finally, a waterfall which emerges from a miniature house and cascades down to the bottom of the great rift. The design makes provision for a completely subterranean road system which explains the need for the enormous volume underground.

This prompted the invention of the great rift: an irregular break in the ground, of varying width, which cuts across the entire project at all levels. This creates an urban dimension for the services and infrastructures located underground, and enhances simple functional spaces with the quality of architecture. The two facades facing each other across the rift are perforated by a regular series of windows, entrances, external staircases, iron footbridges, roads and the underground railway. At the lowest level a narrow pavement divides the winding contour of the buildings from an artificial pond which reflects the distant sky.

With G Grossi

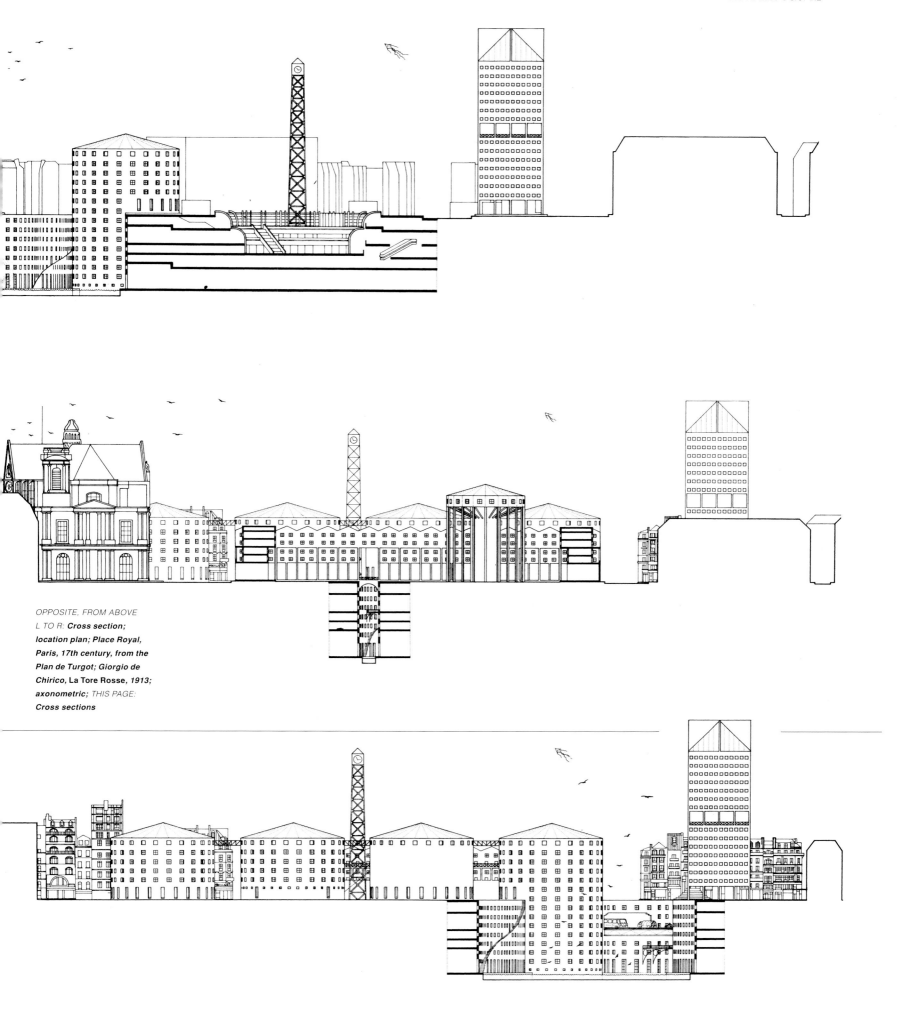

OPPOSITE, FROM ABOVE
L TO R: **Cross section;**
location plan; Place Royal,
Paris, 17th century, from the
Plan de Turgot; Giorgio de
Chirico, **La Tore Rosse,** *1913;*
axonometric; *THIS PAGE:*
Cross sections

 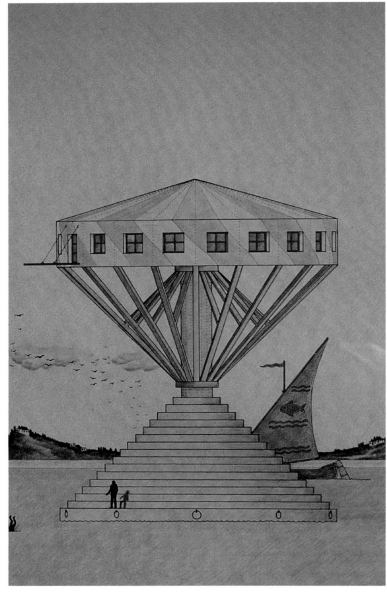

THE ALPINE THEATRE

'The Enigma of Form', 1979-80

The possibility of combining two specific and contrasting motifs in a single construction has fascinated Minardi for a long time: they are Pistocchi's theatre with its understated universalism and the suburban merry-go-round with its noisy indifference – the first destined to create ruins, the latter scrap.

Between the optimism and hope of an empty form and the cynicism and desperation of a solid mechanism, a self-contained machine emerges, able to fulfil its own destiny. This small theatre can be built on the

most varied sites and adapted to its setting through the use of appropriate colours and materials; it can be clad with lead, copper, slate or even painted in bright colours.

*ABOVE, FROM L TO R: **The Alpine Theatre in different settings;** OPPOSITE, BELOW L TO R: **Merry-go-round; Giorgio de Chirico**, La Nostalgia dell'infinito, **1914, detail***

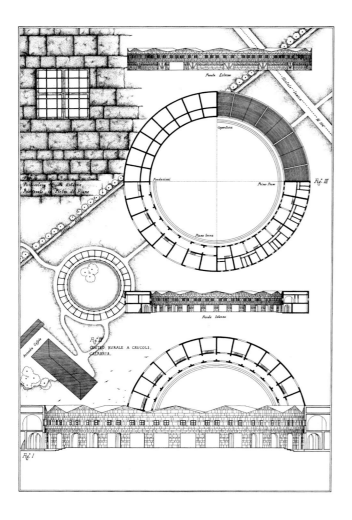

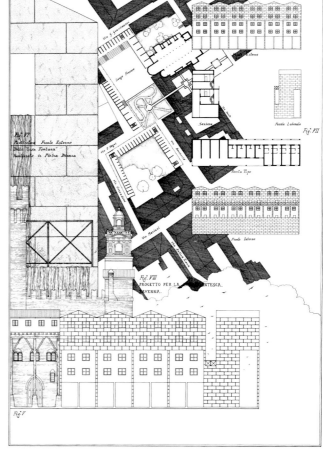

SEVEN DRAWINGS FOR AN EXHIBITION
VENICE BIENNALE, 1980

These drawings, designed for the Venice Biennale, bring together all the characteristic features of Minardi's work. The architectural vocabulary which recurs in his designs, often modified slightly according to location or latitude, determines his structural approach. A wall which closes off a room, a window, a roof with variable pitch according to climate, construction materials chosen according to the surroundings; all are features which determine the repertory for sensible building.

These drawings are graphic compositions which have their origins in different projects. Using various scales of reproduction, each contains various types of drawing in the background: plans, sections and views of the architectural object; an enlarged projection; a construction detail with indications of the facing materials to be used.

With G Grossi

FROM ABOVE, L TO R: **Rural Centre; The Interrupted Houses; The Ubiquitous Housing Tank; The Pylon Tower; The Belvedere and the Huts; The Gran Bar; The Four Winds Tower**

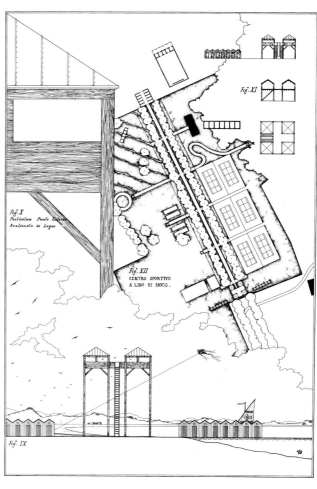

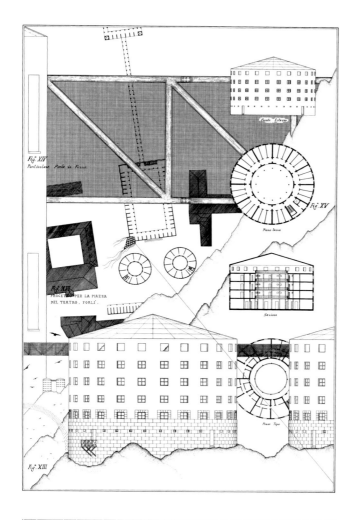

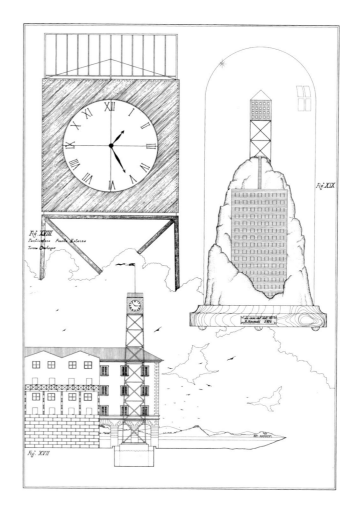

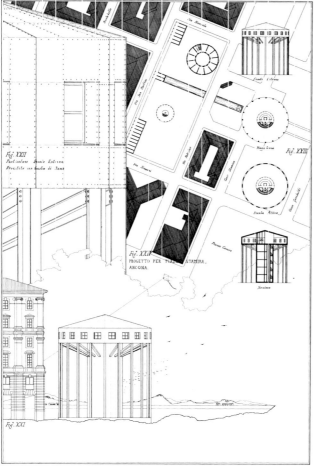

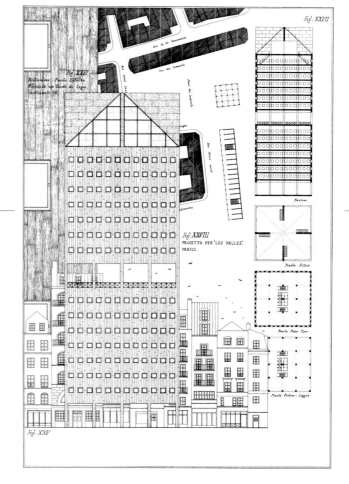

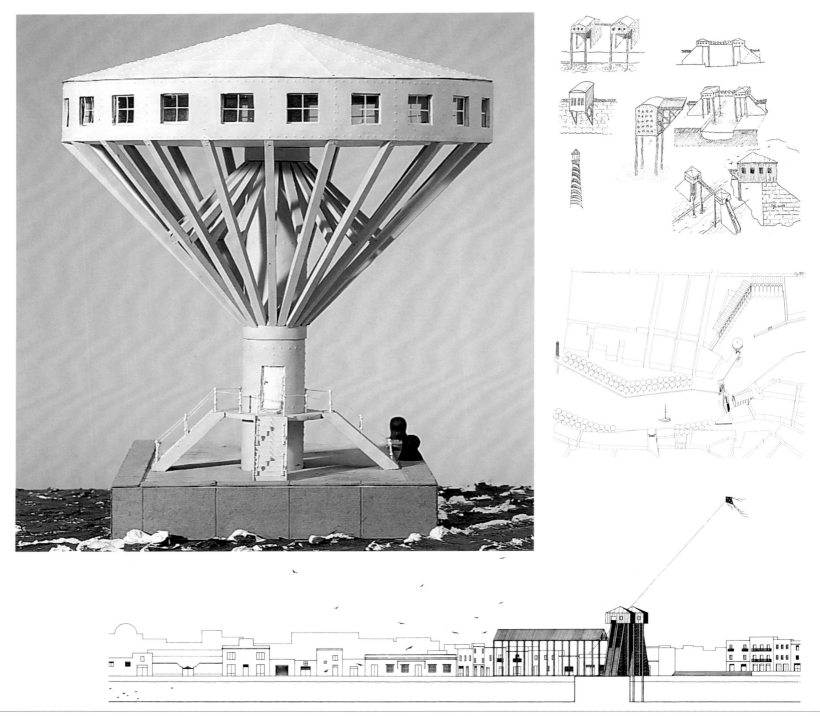

THE CANAL PORT

MAZARA DEL VALLO, SICILY, 1980

Mazara is now the largest fishing port in Italy. An ancient town, it has been ruled successively by the Phoenicians, Romans and Arabs. After AD827, when the Arab occupation began, Mazara became the focal point of the valley in which it stands – surpassing nearby Silenus.

Minardi's project develops initiatives already taken to transfer deep-sea fishing boats to the sea dock by canal, thus freeing the section of river that flows through the town for possible tourist use. The plan is based partly on isolated elements and partly on built spaces within which repeatable building sections can be inserted. Structural details and materials play a key role in the scheme's dialogue with its location: above all the vague suggestion of dock machinery that hangs over the most prominent buildings, such as the drawbridge (which opens to allow sailing boats through), the bar-restaurant made entirely of enamelled metal, the pylon of the lighthouse, and the covered square of the fish market.

With M Casavecchia, F Castagnetti

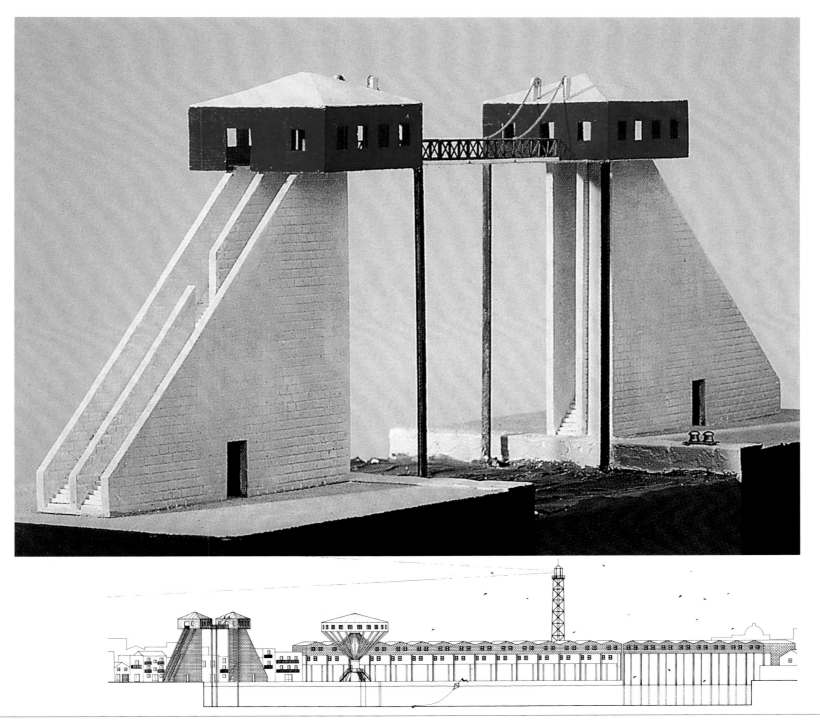

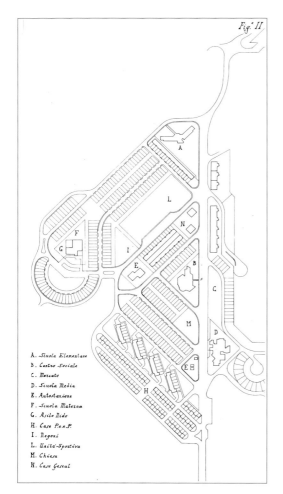

Fig. II

A. Scuola Elementare
B. Centro Sociale
C. Mercato
D. Scuola Media
E. Autostazione
F. Scuola Materna
G. Asilo Nido
H. Case P.e.e.P.
I. Negozi
L. Unità-Sportiva
M. Chiesa
N. Case Gescal

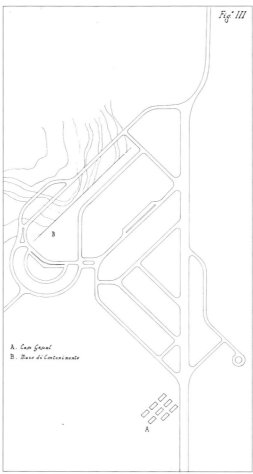

Fig. III

A. Case Gescal
B. Muro di Contenimento

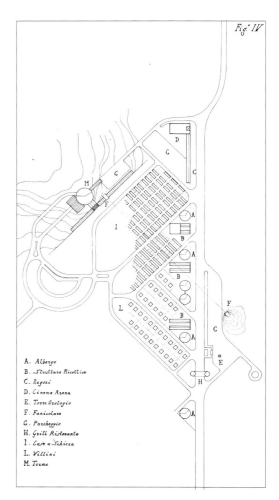

Fig. IV

A. Albergo
B. Strutture Ricettive
C. Negozi
D. Cinema Arena
E. Torre Orologio
F. Funicolare
G. Parcheggio
H. Grill Ristorante
I. Case a Schiera
L. Villini
M. Terme

  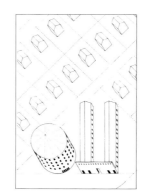 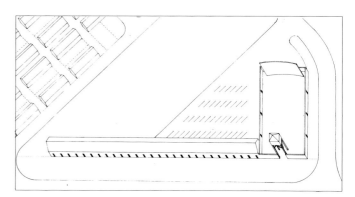

THE SPA TOWN

CALATAFIMI, SICILY, 1980

After the damage caused by the 1968 earthquake, it was decided to relocate a thousand of Calatafimi's six thousand residents in a new settlement on a flat site to the southeast of the existing town. The infrastructure was installed – the proposed network of streets was supplied with sewers, public lighting and footpaths – but the site remained unused and devoid of buildings.

Minardi's project seeks to redesign the area in order to give it an urban appearance and identity. His scheme is based largely on the predetermined street layout (both for reasons of economy and context) and uses the opportunity to present this small town as a spa. Its forms are inspired by those of the existing temporary buildings, the small shed-like houses and the clock tower.

Initially, Minardi wasn't keen to work on the project, being interested not so much in developing or planning a city, as in the study of its smaller elements. He prefers not to predict the whole at the outset, but to leave its development to chance.

With M Casavecchia, F Castagnetti, B Campana, O Amara, A Cupani, R Cristofaro, R Profita, D Piro

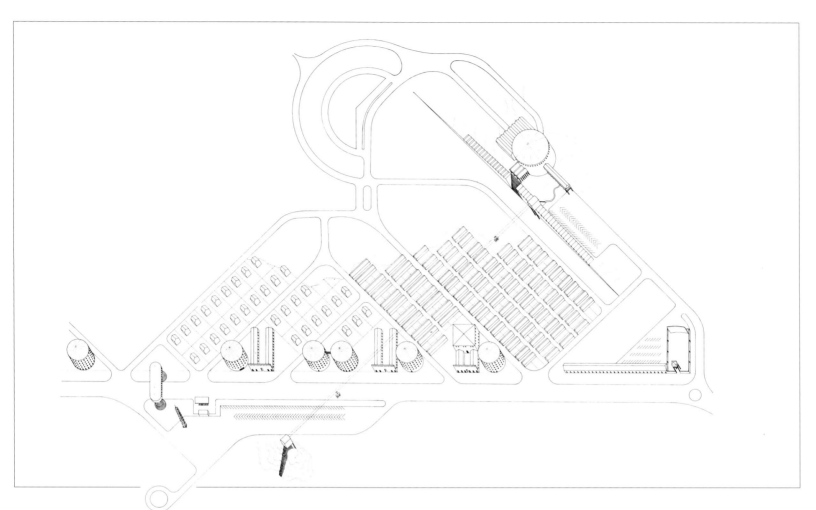

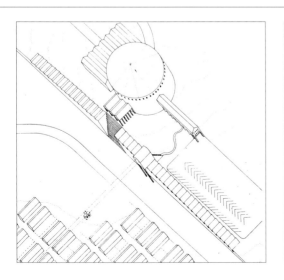 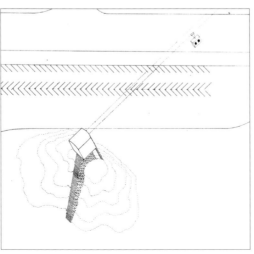

*OPPOSITE, FROM ABOVE L TO R: **Original project proposed by the city council; existing road network; Minardi's proposals; the kursaal and hotel; housing; casino; shops, cinema and arena;** FROM ABOVE L TO R: **Axonometric; temporary housing in which people are accommodated until the completion of a permanent settlement; the spa; cablecar***

87 LEOPOLDSTRASSE

MUNICH, 1981

The interior design company Focus, based in Munich and Berlin, and the Alchymia studio, based in Milan, invited some German and Italian architects to redesign an existing building. The aim was to bring schemes together and compare them in a single architectural exhibition.

In a restrained proposal, Minardi seeks to restore the building and modify it slightly: his objective being to rationalise and recover its original typological and structural schematism. Within this essential framework, the building's various occupants can add their own furnishings and minor modifications.

Externally, the design takes over the existing building through the complex interplay of its parts, based on small additions, on the reconstruction of some perishable elements in permanent materials, and on the use of an appropriate facing material.

With M Casavecchia, E Marraffa

ABOVE: **Details of facade clad in copper and wood;** *OPPOSITE ABOVE:* **Cross section; ground-floor plan and sketches;** *CENTRE:* **A house in Edinburgh; models;** *BELOW:* **Sketches**

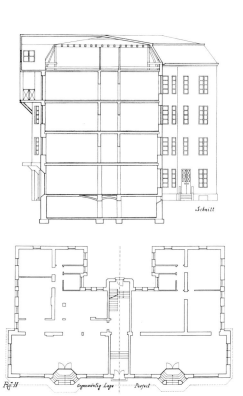

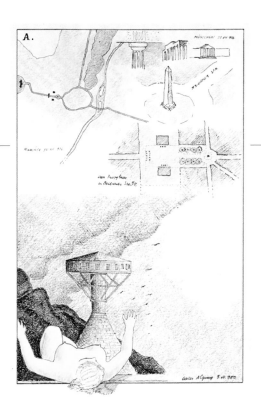

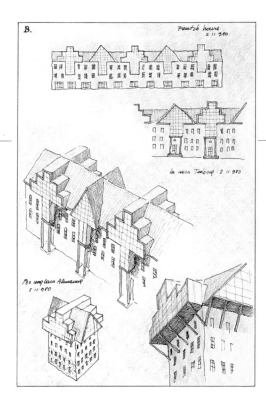

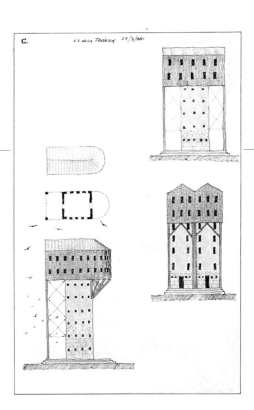

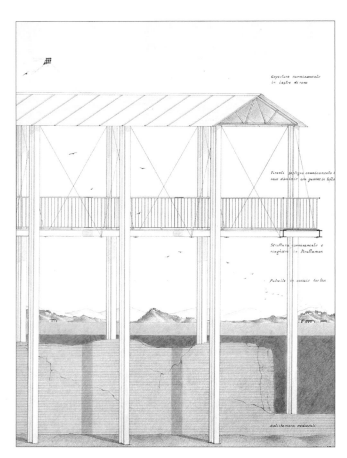

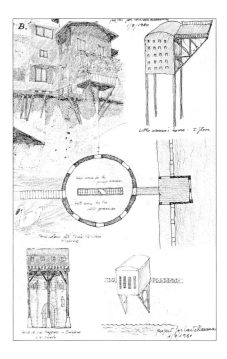

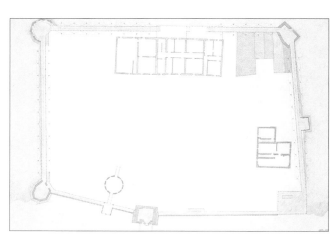

RESTORATION OF THE MALATESTA CASTLE

GATTEO, CESENA, 1981-95

There has been a fortress on the site of the Malatesta Castle since Roman times, though most of what remains now is medieval with the exception of the imposing gateway which is seventeenth century. Minardi's scheme seeks to combine conservation with a functional programme for the whole building. The outer parts of the castle are restored for shops and houses, and the central area is reserved for communal purposes. A small circular tower is planned to house services for the public area, and living quarters for a caretaker. The

encircling walls are restored as a city boundary and in parts as a walkway. In addition to this, the project consists of two main elements: a tower, and roofing and a small bridge.

The cylindrical tower has a single flight of steps on the outside with a metal gangway linking it to the existing walkway on top of the castle walls and an observation post projecting over the moat. The lookout post is supported by iron girders and its walls are made of tarred wooden planks. The old fortifications are covered by a light metal structure – a roof

and connecting bridge held up by stay-bars – except where the walkway on top of the walls is already in operation. This roof, as in archaeological excavation sites, protects the historic fabric while adding a heightened dimension to the whole complex. The suspension bridge provides access to the original walkway. For events in the summer, temporary tiers of wooden seating can be erected from the level of the walkway. The pilasters of the roofing are ideally spaced to support awnings for the weekly market.

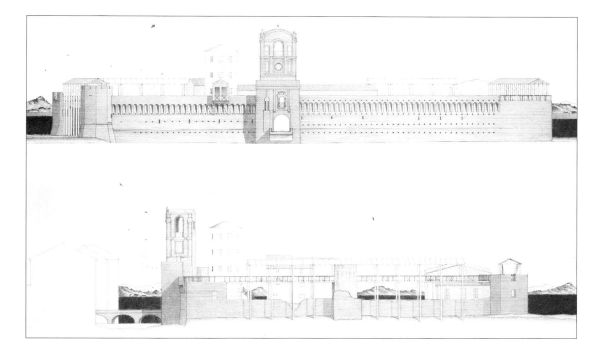

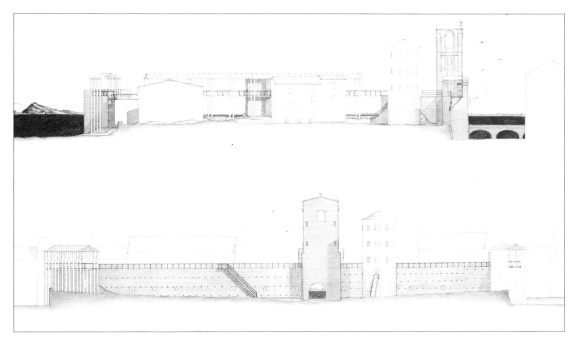

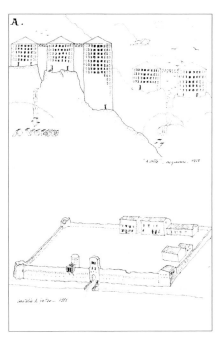

Minardi's scheme draws some of its visual references from the surrounding landscape of the region with its simple volumes and shapes. These include bell towers, dating from the tenth century, which stand alongside ancient Byzantine basilicas; protective roofs of archaeological excavations; and silos and iron-roofed farm buildings which dot the countryside.

(Construction of this project is about to begin at the time of writing.)

With L Capoblanco, P Pezzi, I Rubinetti, S Campana, M Casavecchia, A Olivucci, L Zaganelli, E Brunetti, M Rossi

OPPOSITE, FROM ABOVE
L TO R: **Sketches; elevation of footbridge above castle walls; sketches; 10th-century bell tower of San Apollinare in Classe; site plan; local farm buildings;** *ABOVE LEFT:* **Elevations and cross sections;** *ABOVE RIGHT:* **Sketches;** *OVERLEAF:* **Elevations**

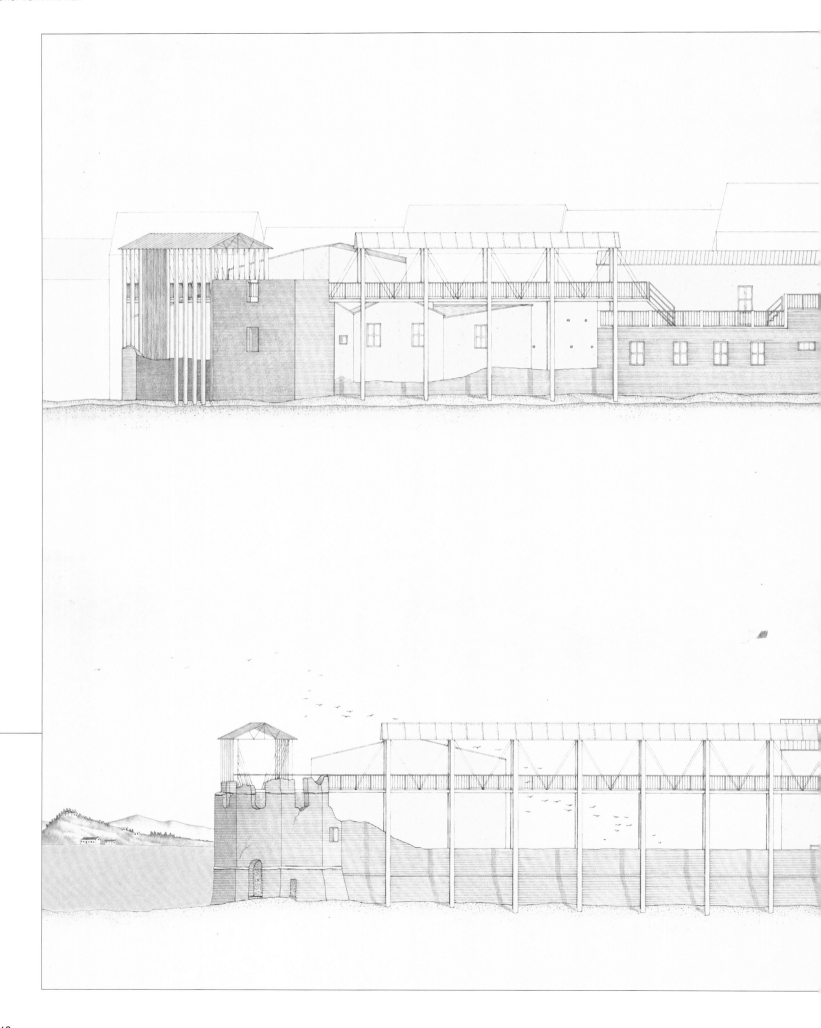

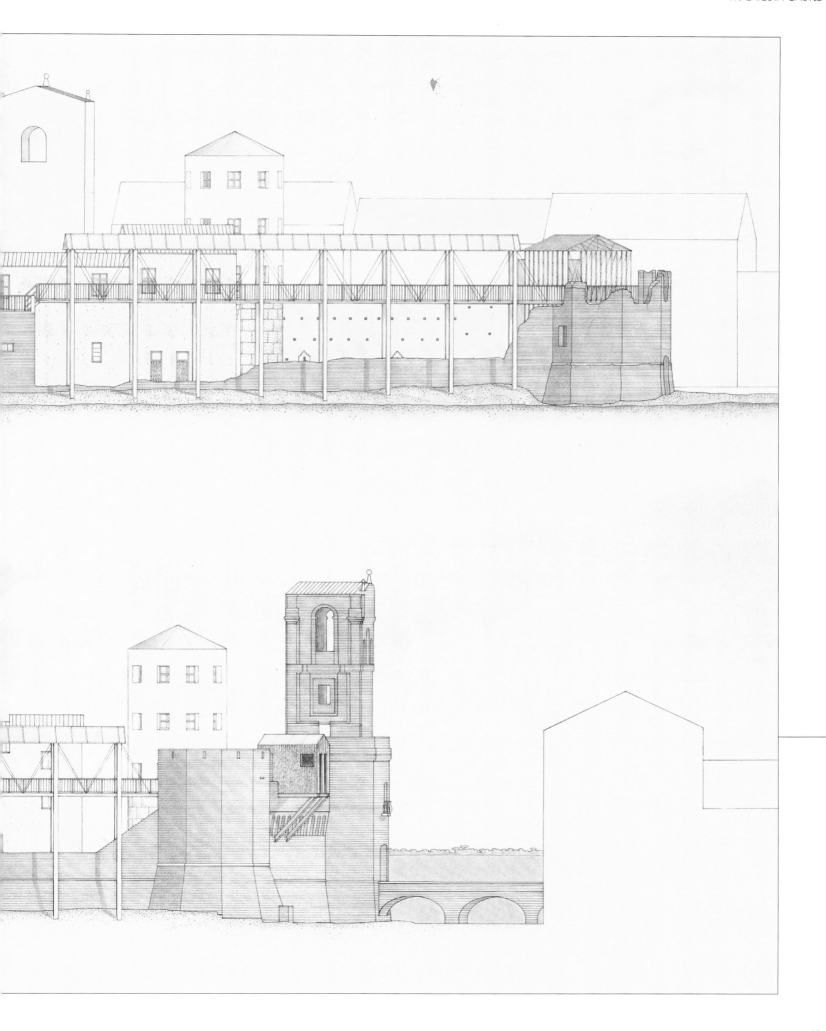

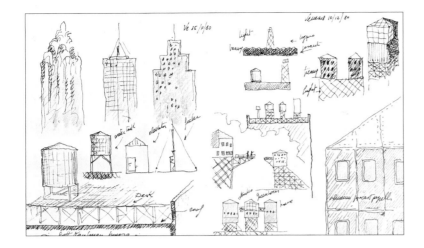 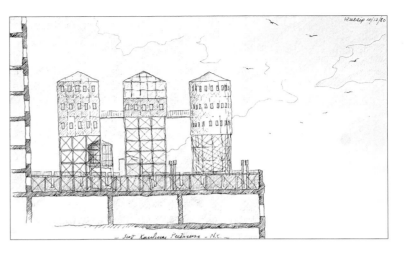

 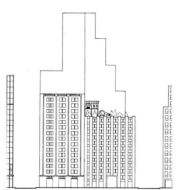 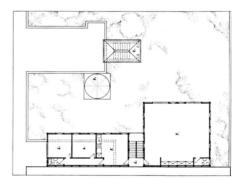 

KAUFMAN HOUSE
PARK AVENUE, NEW YORK, 1981

This penthouse project for Scott Kaufman, a famous designer of racing yachts, is sited on a building facing the corner of Park Avenue and 57th Street, and revolves around a number of fundamental considerations. First, the volumetric arrangement of the project, its use and the character of the site (the tall sill which surmounts the building) mean that this addition cannot be considered as the top of the skyscraper. Second, building regulations in New York prohibit the penthouse directly facing Park Avenue: it has to conform to the alignments regulating the relation between buildings and the street. Third, working conditions on the site call for dry assemblage (if possible) of prefabricated elements rather than traditional methods or craftsmanship.

The plan aims to identify a number of structural elements that can be rested on the building, analogous to the service installations clustered on the roofs of skyscrapers which make such a decisive contribution to the urban landscape: water tanks, radio grids, air-conditioning plant and elevator cabins. In this way architecture turns into an assemblage of components: here the sections of the prefabricated cabin, its supporting pylon structures, and the traditional iron staircases outside.

With M Casavecchia and R Libralon

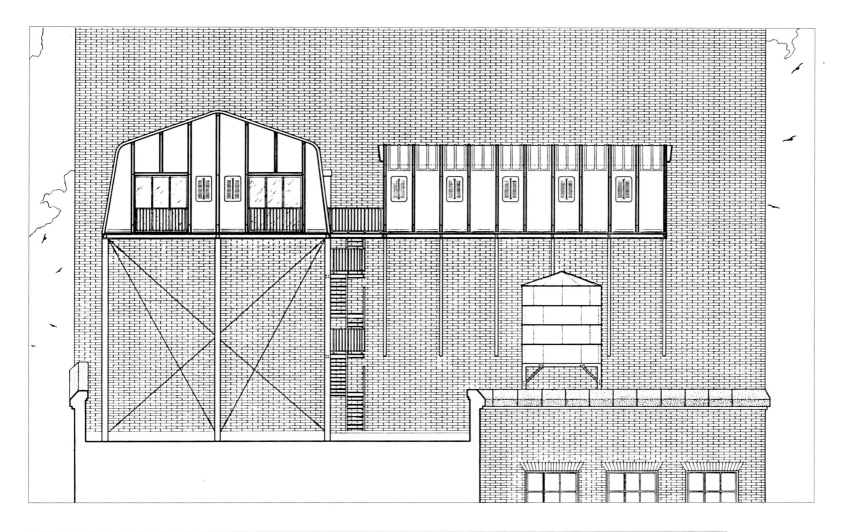

OPPOSITE, FROM ABOVE
L TO R: **Sketches; water tank;
elevation of block; plan of
penthouse; prefabricated huts;**
LEFT: **Elevations**

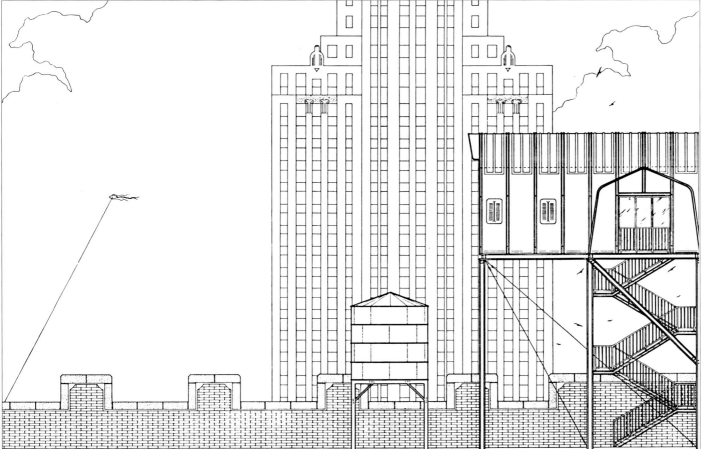

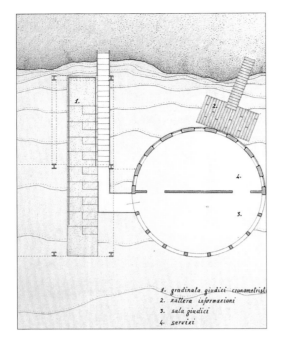
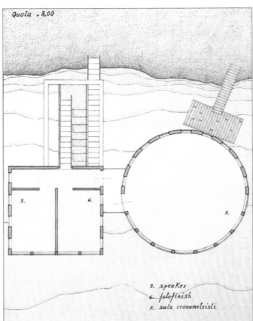
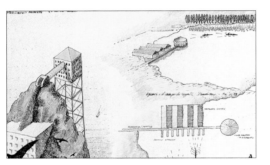

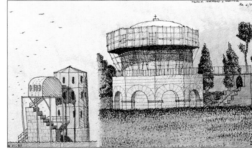
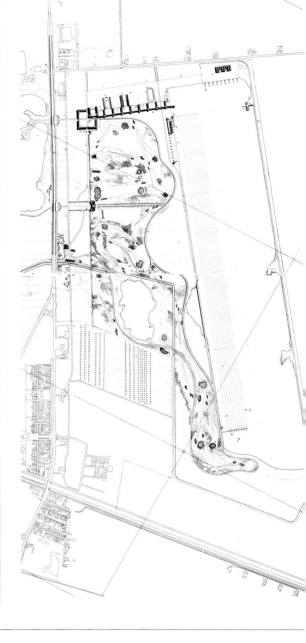

STANDIANA PARK CANOEING FACILITIES

RAVENNA, 1983

Minardi's project for Standiana Park includes facilities for golf, cycling, tennis, swimming and canoeing. For canoeing there is an artificial lake measuring 2,500 by 500 metres, a sports village, equipment specifically for international competitions with grandstands, annexes and a finish line tower.

This tower, which occupies a very small space, fulfils a number of closely related functions and its design has been shaped by the requirements of the sport. It is necessary for the nine judges to sit on steps aligned exactly with the finish line in order to adjudicate the results. The photofinish must also be on this line and to one side a speaker. Connected to the steps there has to be a judges' room and an information display for the contestants. The timekeeper's room has to be sited to ensure close connections with the photofinish. Thus, the building intentionally expresses the complexity and extreme specialisation of its role.

With G Grossi, P Nicolin, F Purini

*FROM ABOVE: **Plans of the jury tower; sketches; site plan;** OPPOSITE, FROM ABOVE: **Section through jury tower and boatsheds; local sheds; floating dredge; section through jury tower and spectators' stand***

Fig. VII

1983

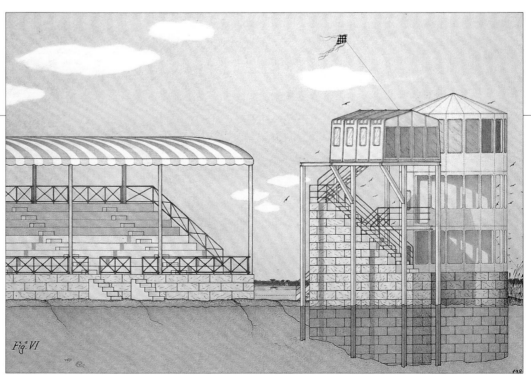

Fig. VI

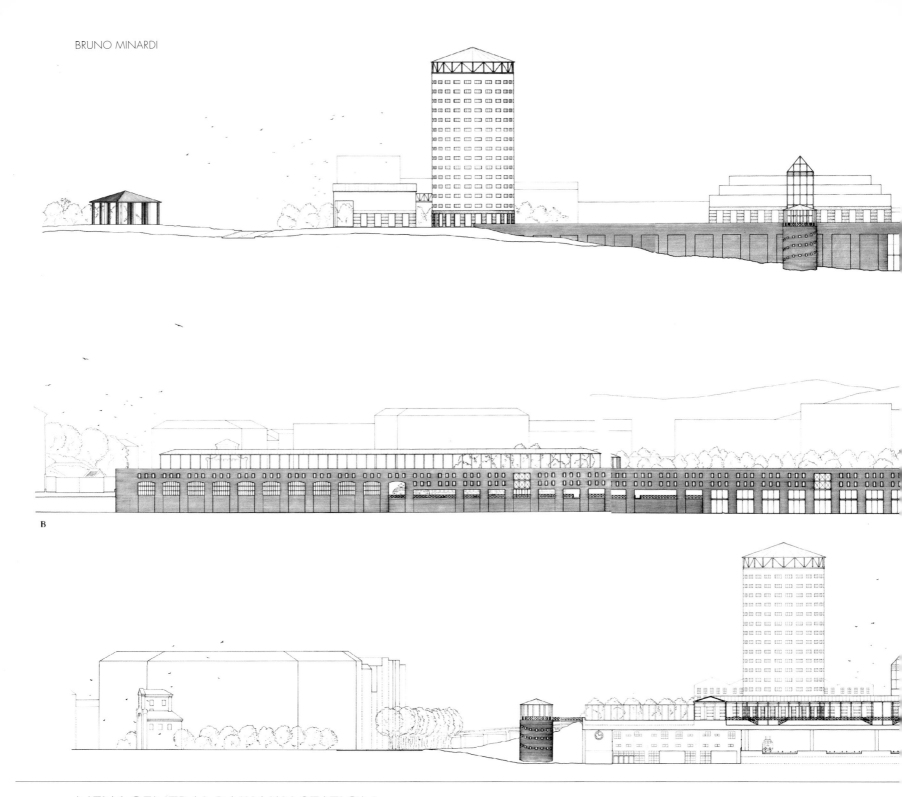

B

NEW CENTRAL RAILWAY STATION

BOLOGNA, 1983

This scheme locates the new station at the level of the existing subway, with the possibility of a secondary entrance on the northern side. A large roof (600 by 150 metres) covers the platforms and has openings for lighting and air circulation; it can be built without interrupting train services. The roof rises 8 metres above current street level, though, with its greenery and trees, it is connected in such a way as to appear to be at ground level, thus becoming a continuation of the North Park towards Montagnola Park.

Minardi proposes clearing the strip of ground above the platforms in order to site public facilities there. These include a large hotel and restaurant, located in a cylindrical tower on the edge of the driveway; a shopping centre with a high, glass-covered mall in the centre, located on the main route across the city; and a square bordered by porticos, located at the eastern end of the park over the station, to accommodate the local weekly markets.

With L Benevolo, G Barbini, L Bonagiunti, U Camerino, R d'Agostino, G Gambirasio, G Grossi, G Lombardi, G Predieri, G Zenoni, A Benevolo, D Favaron, M Gin, E Marraffa

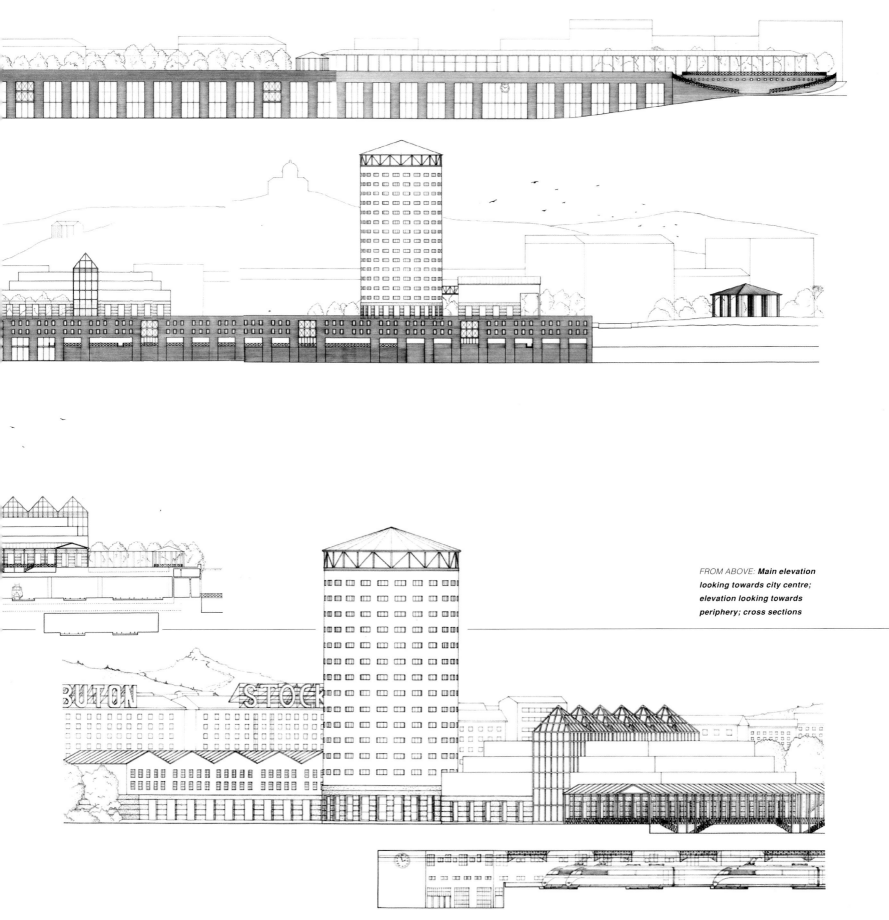

*FROM ABOVE: **Main elevation
looking towards city centre;
elevation looking towards
periphery; cross sections***

THE EUROPEAN TOWN

1984

Minardi's European town was inspired by Hadrian's Villa at Tivoli, where an incredible collection of architectural fragments, gathered from a lifetime's travels, have now become mellowed by time – their images blended. Minardi's vision of the European town is a realistic urban panorama; it is built in an imaginary place with real designs, a few of which actually have been built. Here one can live and work: there are houses, schools, hotels, museums, places of work and entertainment and bridges. The many constituent designs were created by a variety of architects who speak different languages but who are united by one inescapable fact: they are contemporaries.

With E Marraffa

FROM ABOVE: **The European Town,** *pen and ink and pastel,*
45 × 130cm; Giovanni Rossini, **Reconstruction of Campo**
Marzio, 1824

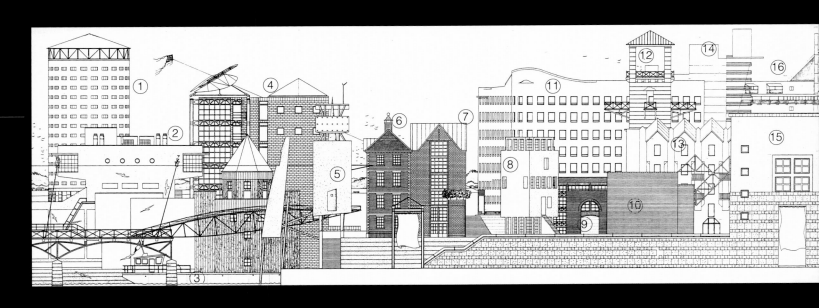

1 *Grossi and Minardi, Grand Hotel, Bologna, 1983; 2 Gustav Peichl, Dépurateur, Berlin, 1981; 3 Aldo Rossi, Teatro del Mondo, Venice, 1980; 4 Joseph Paul Kleihues, Municipal Archives, Solingen, 1981; 5 Peter Wilson, Le Pont des Arts, Paris, 1982; 6 Quinlan Terry, 10 South Square, Gray's Inn,* *London, 1970; 7 Adolfo Natalini, house at 4 Saalgasse, Frankfurt, 1981; 8 OM Ungers, family residence, Hamburg, 1976; 9 Rob Krier, residential apartments, Berlin, 1977/80; 10 Mario Botta, artists' studios, Balerna, 1977/79; 11 Alvaro Siza, building in Kreuzberg, Berlin, 1982; 12 Leon Krier, École* *Saint-Quentin, Yvelines, 1978; 13 Reichling and Reinhardt, Kochstrasse, Berlin, 1980; 14 Rem Koolhaas, towers, Rotterdam, 1980/83; 15 James Stirling, Staatsgalerie, Stuttgart, 1977; 16 Ralph Erskine, Byker, Newcastle-Upon-Tyne, 1970/80*

NEW ICE STADIUM AND SPORTS FACILITIES

CORTINA D'AMPEZZO, 1984

This project called for the reorganisation of a vast site which included the Ice Palace, the Ravalle cablecar landing stage, and the neighbouring area near the River Boite. Minardi's project for this popular resort in the Italian Alps consists of three parts: a bridge and underground garage, an ice rink, a hotel and a sports centre. The bridge over the Boite connects the cablecar terminus with the large underground garage adjoining the Olympic stadium. The main pedestrian route is provided with shops, tourist offices and self-service restaurants at street level. The bridge – a combination of masonry and wood – is a complex multi-purpose structure, being in turn a city gate through which main roads pass; a stone building which descends below ground to the garage; and, in its central part, a real bridge over the river.

The new stadium retains the existing structure which is now an integral part of the Cortina panorama; it is partially underground and its roof extends over the large ice rink. Towards the south a containing dolomite wall serves as the base and front of the new addition. The hotel and sports centre are placed on the slope down to the River Boite in a complex consisting of three parts: the cylindrical tower of the hotel, the base of the hall, and the sports facilities.

Co-architects: G Brusati, R d'Agostino, G Grossi, G Lombardi, G Predieri

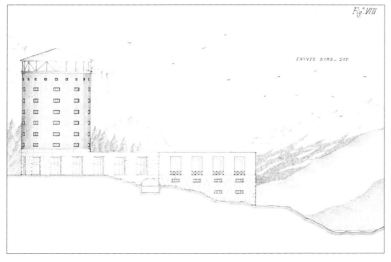

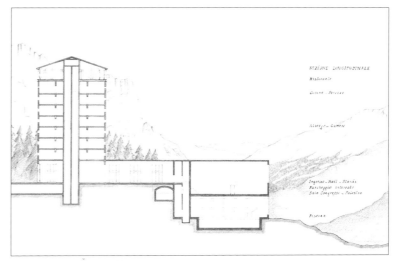

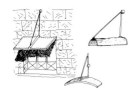

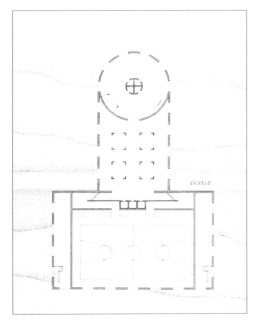

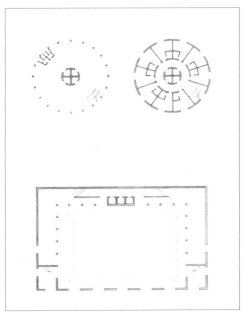

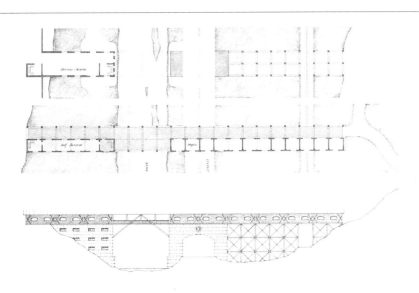

OPPOSITE, FROM ABOVE L TO R: **Bird's-eye views; sketches;**
local wooden house; site plan; grain silo; FROM ABOVE, L TO R:
Elevation and section of hotel and gymnasium; sketches; plan
of hotel and gymnasium; Andrea Palladio's bridge in
Bassano, 16th century; plan of hotel and swimming pool; plan
and elevation of bridge, sketches

59

FROM ABOVE: **Principal elevation of ice stadium; the new doors of the ice stadium**

FROM ABOVE: **South elevation; detail of the bridge**

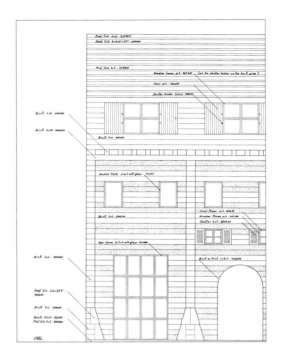

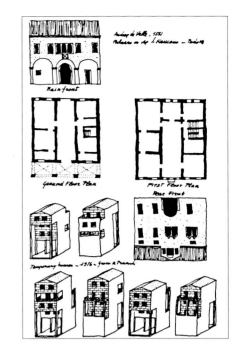

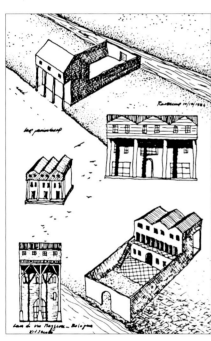

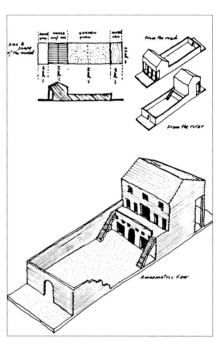

LEGO HOUSE

1984

Minardi's Lego House was produced for an exhibition at the Pompidou Centre in Paris, promoted by Lego Group, in which ten architects each designed a house built from Lego elements. His project is for a villa in an urban context, surrounded by other buildings. The two detached facades face a street and a canal; a portico forms the transitional element on the street side and a sheltered private garden, or courtyard, on the canal side.

The house incorporates a number of factors that contribute to an orderly and happy life: its situation is urban, close to facilities, schools and shops; it has a garden, so that its occupants can spend their siesta outside; and finally it has two shops in its entrance which the owner can rent out or use as workshops, a feature typical of dwellings in classical cities.

OPPOSITE: **Sketches; detail of
main facade; model of house
in Lego bricks, 54 × 133 ×
57cm;** FROM ABOVE, L TO R:
**Facade facing road; facade
facing courtyard; perspective
view; plans**

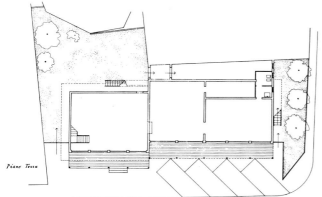

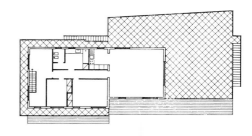

'PUNTO VELA' COMMERCIAL BUILDING

MARINA DI RAVENNA, 1984

This project extends and adds upper floors to a small building, which is occupied by a shop selling sports equipment and sailing accessories, and an agency organising the design of sailing boats for regattas, as well as a small section containing guest rooms.

It faces a large square near the port, from which there are views of the sea, the boats moored along the quay, the lighthouse and, occasionally, the outline of a large merchant ship moving silently along the canal. These local features shape the design which is sympathetic to the forms, materials and colours of its surroundings. Minardi was also influenced by the fishing cabins which are suspended by metal frames on the break-water of the port; the wooden and panelled buildings which peep out from the nearby pine wood; the whites and greys of the coast-guard boats; the wooden railings of the beach cabins; and the metal stairways of the ships.

With G Grossi, M Lucca, G Pezzi, F Poggioli

FROM ABOVE, L TO R:

Perspective view; ground floor plan; fishing cabin; first floor plan

THE WANDERING YARD

ROME, 1985

After an invitation to participate in a design workshop for the historic centre of Rome, Minardi avoided designing a new building, being convinced that the ancient city needed careful restoration and maintenance instead.

Consequently, he devised a movable machine for cleaning monuments.

The machine, designed with the help of Peter Wilson, consists of two separate parts: the cleaning tower and the clean wall machine. The cleaning tower consists of a load-bearing metal structure which stands on an iron framework anchored to a movable platform. The galvanised zinc panels which cover the exterior leave a vertical opening at the front. Once the machine is positioned against a building cleaning and maintenance work can be easily carried out.

The clean wall machine, also resting on a movable platform, has a polished steel face on one side and on the other a wooden structure at the centre of which a large wheel moves two retractable ladders up and down. Beside the wheel there are some items of equipment including a water spray collector with water tank, sprayers and spotlights for possible nightwork.

The tower and machine can be closed together when not in use, joining the steel face of one to the open side of the other. In this position of apparent rest they can instead clean each other.

With P Wilson

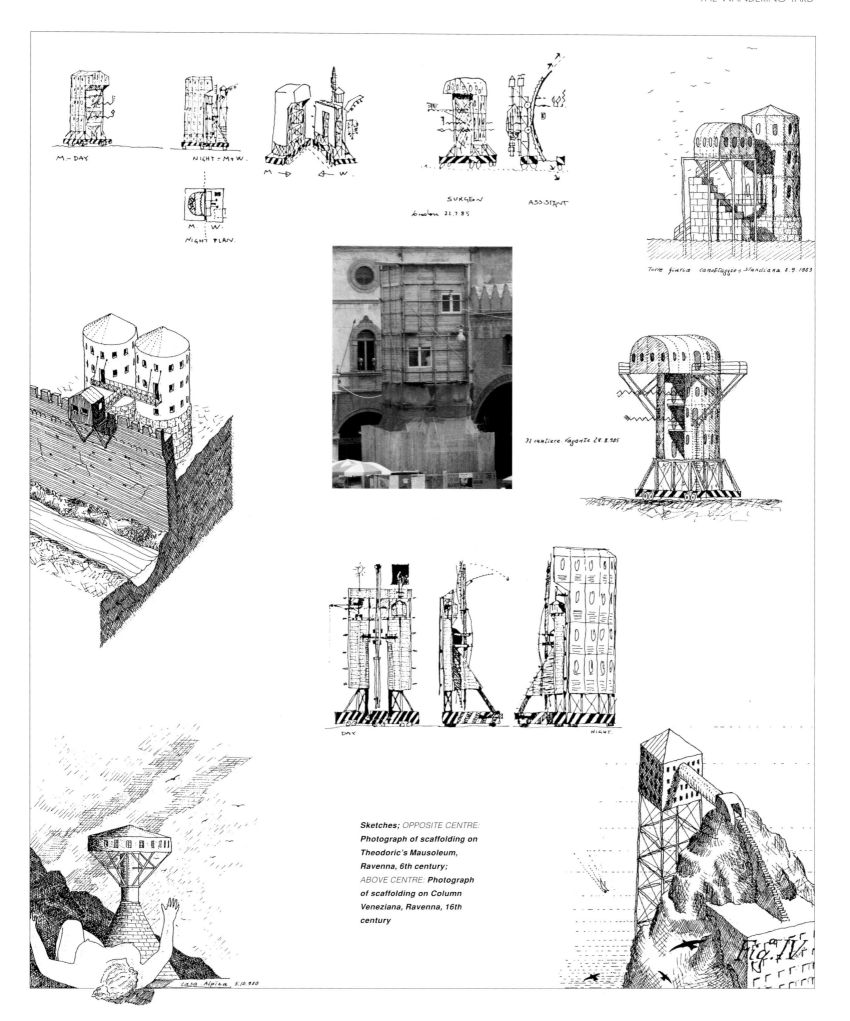

Sketches; OPPOSITE CENTRE:
Photograph of scaffolding on
Theodoric's Mausoleum,
Ravenna, 6th century;
ABOVE CENTRE: Photograph
of scaffolding on Column
Veneziana, Ravenna, 16th
century

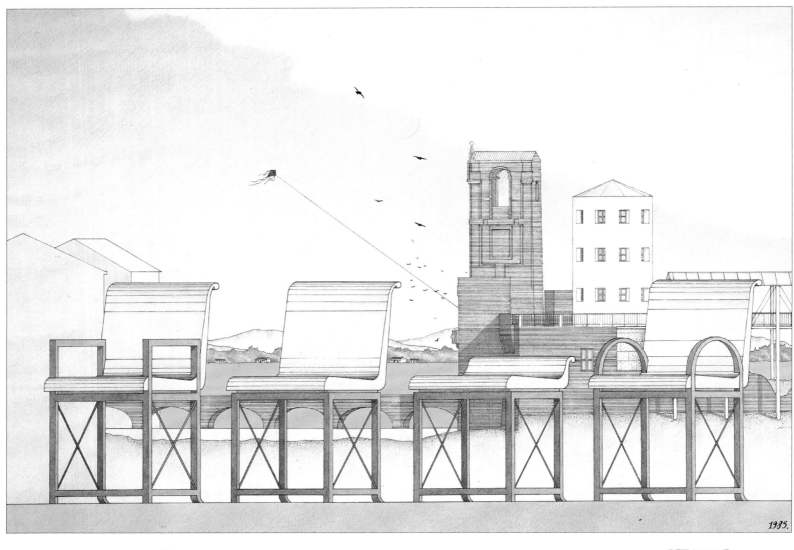

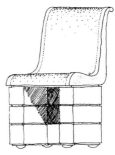

THE SAGITTARIA CHAIR

1984-85

The basic concept of this design is the superimposition of a sinuous organic element, the seat, on a rigid geometrical form, the structure. The impression of duality – with no attempt at reconciliation – is a theme which has always run through Minardi's work: above and below, old and new, solid and fragile, artificial and natural.

He has often designed sequences in which the same building appears on different backgrounds: hills, sea, countryside and city. Sometimes the building changes slightly according to context, in its colour, facing material, or the way it touches the ground.

Following this method of approach, Marco Buzzoni – for whom Minardi designed the Sagittaria chair – took a series of photographs. In so doing, he fused elements from Minardi's figurative and emotional vocabularies, such as the kite and the bull-terrier, in his own intuitive way – for example, in the countryside of Parma or in a ray of sunlight in a dark church: images from a dream. Finally, like all things which linger in time waiting to be finished, chance and coincidence have done the rest.

Thanks to Gaia de Beaumont for having kindly made available his lovely Zuffi.

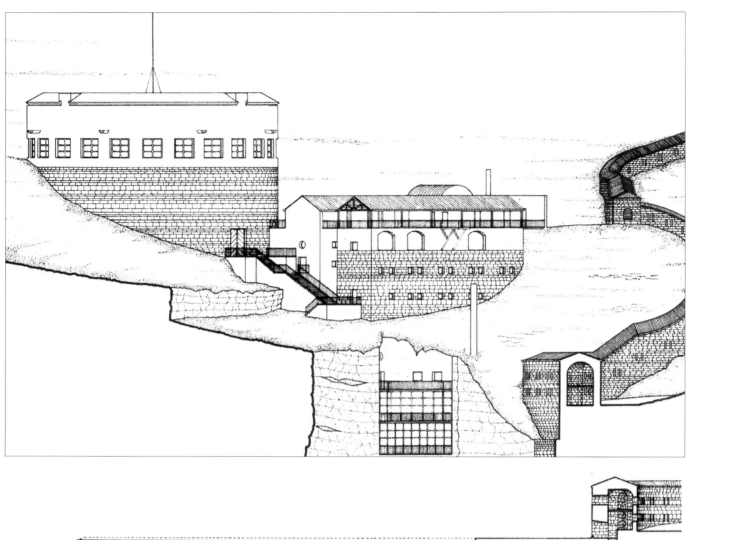

FROM ABOVE: **South elevation;**
sections of the restored
fortress; OPPOSITE, FROM
ABOVE: **Plan of the museum;**
section through main gallery

FIRST WORLD WAR MUSEUM

PRIMOLANO, BELLUNO, 1988

The Tagliata di Primolano fort, near Mount Grappa, was an important strategic point during World War I. A large museum was proposed to commemorate this, sited inside the fort, and housing reconstructions of battles and examples of arms, artillery and planes.

In this degree project by Enrico Pietrogrande, one of Minardi's pupils, the museum fits comfortably within the existing fortifications. The galleries – often underground, like the trenches and tunnels of war time – create an intriguing route between the museum and the

fortress. The nucleus of the museum is a large cylindrical tower, partly underground and modern in style. This is the hub of museum activities and appears as a kind of castle within a castle. To one side two parallel buildings with sloping roofs house a bar/restaurant, the caretaker's lodgings and guest rooms. A study centre and conference hall are included in the plans, standing adjacent to the museum, to house lectures, debates and source material.

Degree project by Enrico Pietrogrande, Venice University, supervised by Bruno Minardi

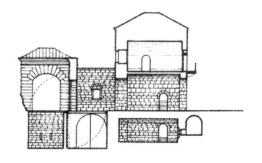

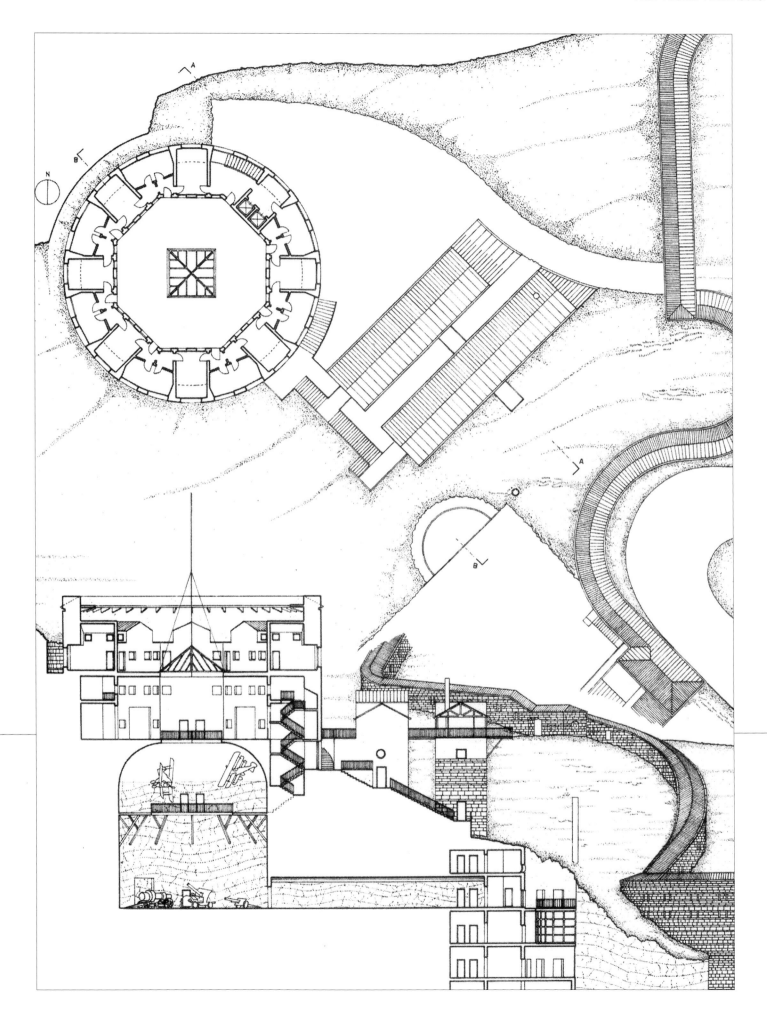

GENS CLAUDIA

GARDEN FURNITURE, 1985

Minardi conceived this furniture – a table with chairs, an armchair, a coffee table, a *dormeuse* and a *guéridon* – as possible furnishings for a place that is not necessarily

a garden, but one which can transform into a terrace or even an interior with a similar feel. In its light elegance, he seeks to attain an understated classicism which goes beyond the style more common for this type of furniture. It is designed in enamelled iron, or steel with a brushed matt finish, with flat, perforated surfaces as is usual for outdoor furniture. In some cases there are enlarged oak leaves which enhance the ingenious natural effect.

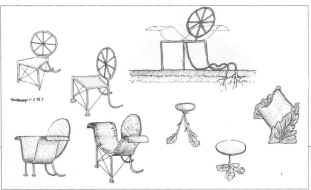

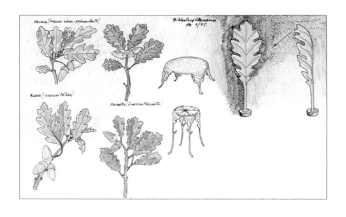

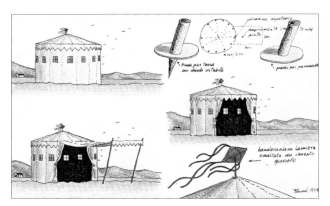

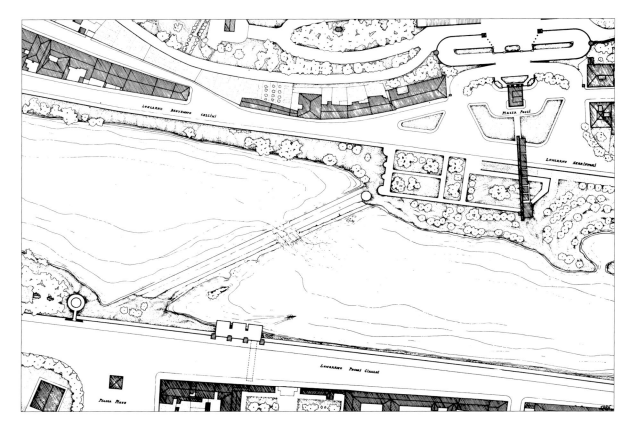

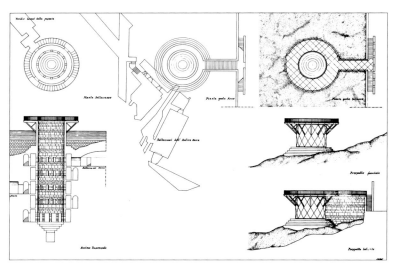

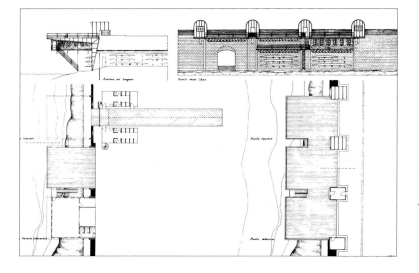

SAN NICCOLO FISH WEIR

FLORENCE, 1986

An important area in Florence is where the city's streets meet the River Arno opposite the San Niccolo Fish Weir. The old city adapted itself to the river with houses and workshops joined along its banks, sometimes extending into the water – a complicated arrangement with unique features, interrupted elements, fragments and layers. This was certainly more congenial than the compact solution envisaged and partly realised in the nineteenth century.

Minardi's plan, created for the Milan Triennale, responds to the old city and consists of the

three distinct features: a boathouse, an 'underground tower' and a guesthouse.

The boathouse, built entirely in iron and wood, consists of large terraces and a restaurant supported by large corbels overhanging the Arno. Under the terraces there is a tunnel, open at one end, containing moorings for the boats and related facilities.

The 'underground tower' is a tower turned inside out, like a glove, and sunk into the ground: the outside thus becomes the hollow cylinder which defines the interior. The stairs

descend to the subterranean floors of the old Mint and lead to a tunnel (once used for pipes) under the Fish Weir and on to the Piazza Poggi.

The guesthouse is distinguished by a large *pietra serena* wall which crosses the Lungarno Serristori and ends almost in the river. Inside there is a complicated system of stairs and passages, like a vertical labyrinth; outside there are wooden service buildings and various rooms in iron and wood.

With M Lucca, G Pezzi, F Poggioli

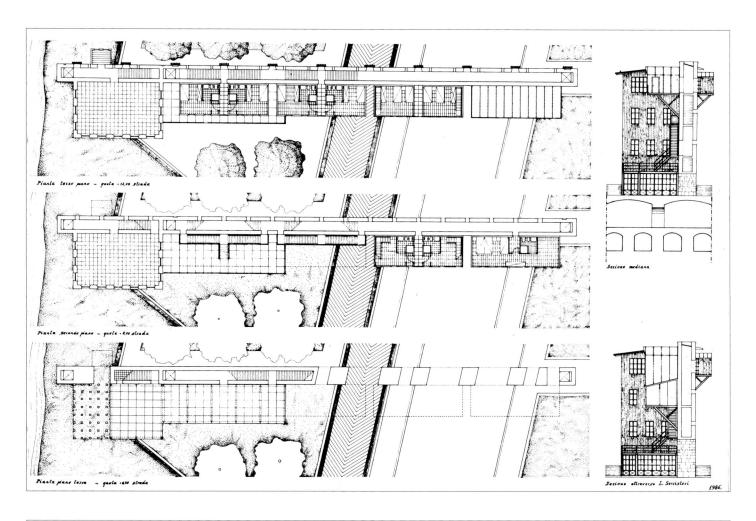

Pianta terzo piano ~ quota +12,00 strada

Pianta secondo piano ~ quota +8,90 strada

Pianta piano terra ~ quota +4,00 strada

Sezione mediana

Sezione attraverso L. Serristori   1986.

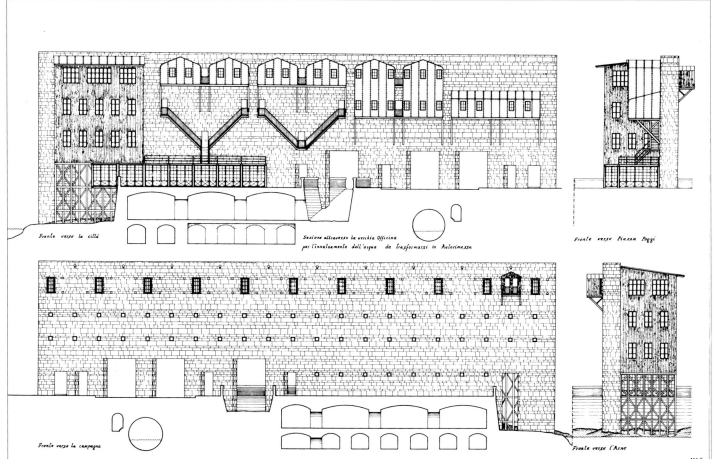

Fronte verso la città

Sezione attraverso la vecchia Officina
per l'innalzamento dell'acqua da trasformarsi in Autorimessa

Fronte verso Piazza Poggi

Fronte verso la campagna

Fronte verso l'Arno

1986.

OPPOSITE, FROM ABOVE
L TO R: **Site plan; Giovanni**
Fantozzi, view of the River
Arno, 18th century; Giotto,
Expelling the Devils from
Arezzo, 14th century, detail;
plans and sections of under-
ground tower; *ABOVE:* **Plans,**
sections and elevations of
guesthouse

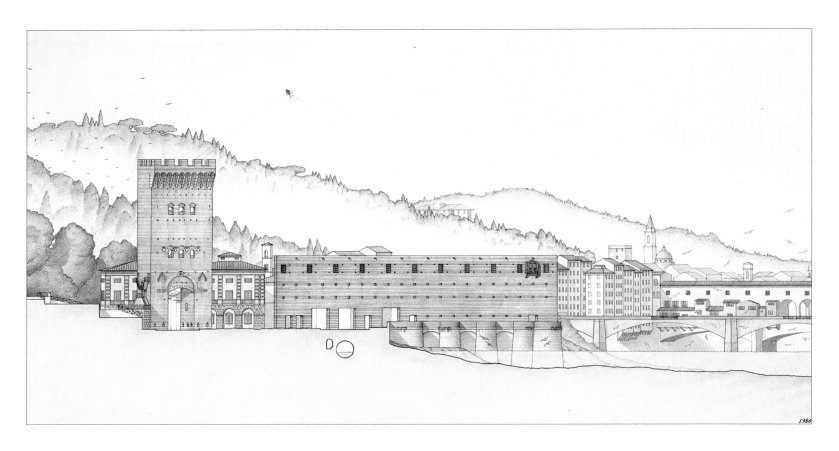

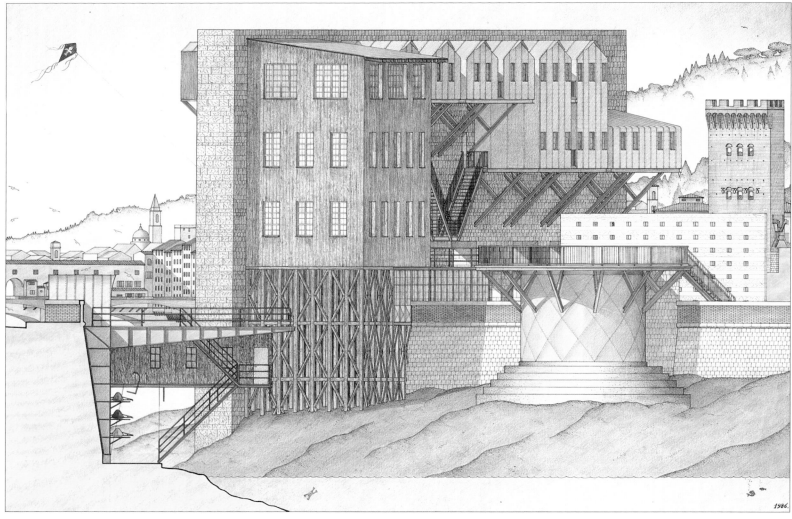

ABOVE: **Sections**; *BELOW:* **Elevation of guest house; model of guest house with old tower**

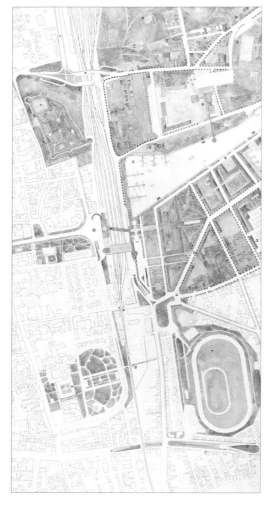
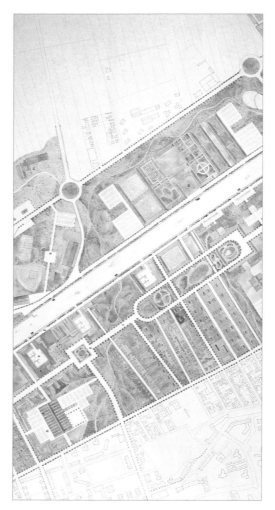

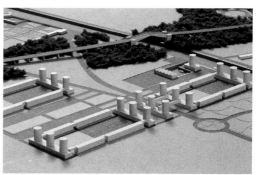

MARMARICA: REDEVELOPMENT OF OLD HARBOUR

RAVENNA, 1989

Minardi's Marmarica project is centred around the reclamation of a large plot of land, left mainly unused by the industrial port, for urban development. In Ravenna, as in other towns, the demand for specialised services and new spaces has led to the abandonment of the oldest part of the industrial port-canal in favour of more extensive sites further away, with better connections to the sea and railways.

Minardi proposes both to restore and improve existing buildings which are of importance to the area's industrial history, as well as to construct new buildings and roads in order to reorganise the site for a more urban application.

With new homes, university and port administration, sports and cultural centres, squares, tree-lined streets and new quays for tourist use, the redevelopment area will become a large new quarter expanding naturally. Its new use will be more environmentally friendly and it will not treat the city as a place of unstoppable expansion.

With G Grossi, M Casadio

FROM ABOVE: **Master plans;**
models looking towards sea;
city centre; existing site;
OPPOSITE, FROM ABOVE
L TO R: **Drawbridge linking**
development other areas of
the city; model showing
university and new resort; the
drawbridge; model looking
towards the town

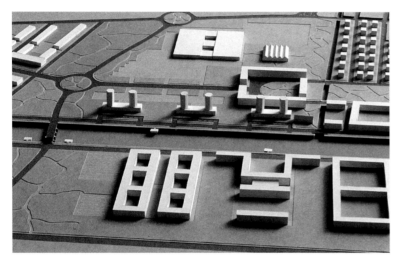

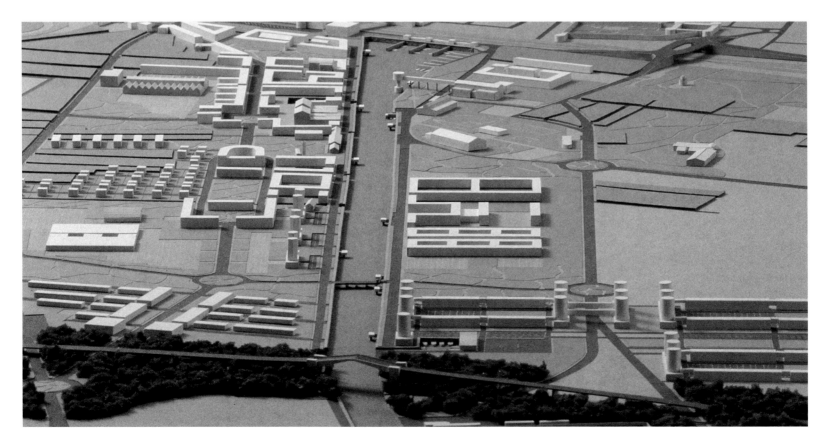

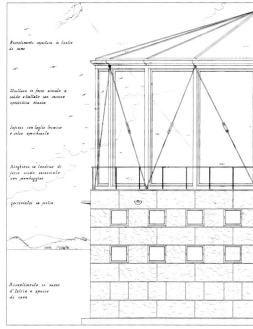

SAR TRANSPORTI OFFICES

RAVENNA, 1987

The project involved adding to and adapting the premises of a large haulage firm on the outskirts of Ravenna, near the outer ring road. Situated in the centre of an immense tarmac yard, used as a parking area for hundreds of articulated lorries, the building lies on an invisible divide between town and country.

The plan centres around creating offices and a committee conference room in the existing building. The extension that this required suggested a large insect-like creation to Minardi: the conference room forming the head; the pillars, the feet; the new roof placed on the old part, the wing-cover; the tube for the air conditioning, the antennas; and the sheet metal, a soft underbelly.

Apart from this rather extravagant conception, which has given the project its final form, the building developed quickly following its own architectural laws and criteria.

As at the Cesena council houses, the Malatesta Castle, and the project for the San Niccolo Fish Weir, Minardi worked around a high-tech structure, aiming to recycle existing prefabricated material, focusing more on the surrounding industrial landscape than the architectural style of the old town.

With M Fabio, M Lucca, F Poggioli, F Colletti, G Salotti

*FROM ABOVE: **Detail of facade; Theodoric's Mausoleum, Ravenna, 6th century; simple barn roofs***

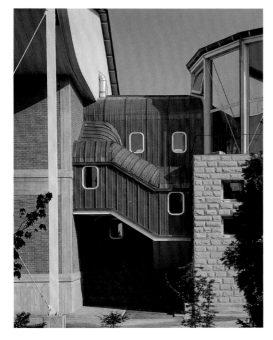

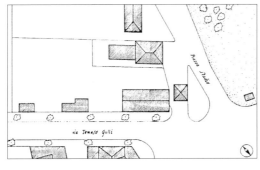
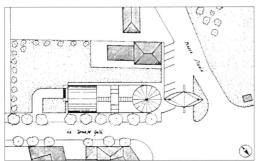

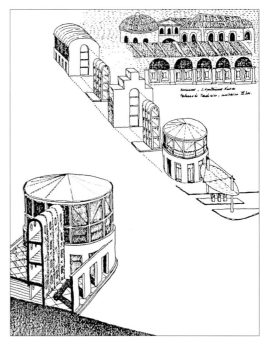
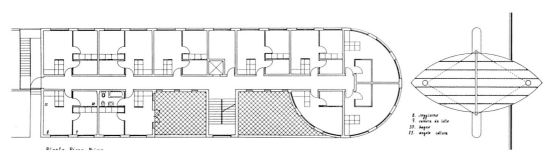

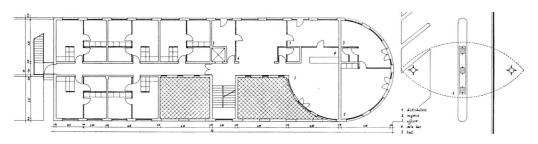

MEDIMAR HOUSE

RAVENNA, 1990

Medimar House is located on the corner of two streets in the outskirts of Ravenna, near the railway station and the industrial port. The surroundings are characteristic of the fragmentary mediocrity of all growing areas, something the design cannot and does not attempt to remedy or even less, to modify. Rather, Minardi tried to produce a dialogue between features of the old and new parts of the city. Having considered the processes of overlaying various architectural elements, he worked out a way to recover ideas from industrial architecture and its extraordinary archaeology.

Medimar House arises from a need for temporary accommodation for port officials and industrial staff with centralised services and an underground car park. In the forecourt the petrol station has a completely revised layout with a striking leaf-shaped shelter.

With G Grossi, L Zaganelli

FROM ABOVE, L TO R: **Site plans before the project and with the project; sketches; first floor plan; ground floor plan; view of model; 6th-century mosaic showing Imperial Palace, Ravenna;** *OPPOSITE, ABOVE:* **Perspective view from courtyard;** *CENTRE AND BELOW:* **Perspective views from square**

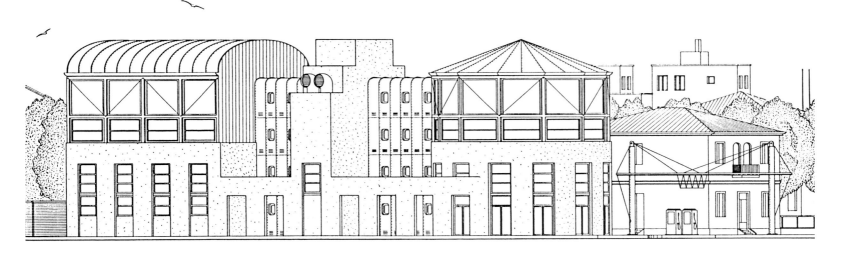

THE MOSAIC HOUSE, ST CROCE

RAVENNA, 1987

Mosaics, like frescos, are never independent of the buildings in which they are found: architecture and decoration are a single entity. Minardi's project is designed with this in mind. He thought of a small house attached to the interior wall of a church as if it were the hut of a shipyard, or the place from which a priest might appear or where a baby could be hidden. The idea of extension, addition and growth through time is a recurrent theme in his work (as has already been seen in his projects for council houses in Cesena, Leopoldstrasse

87, the Malatesta Castle, the new ice stadium in Cortina, the San Niccolo Fish Weir in Florence, and the SAR offices in Ravenna). Past and present, old and new, the superimposition of new elements on existing buildings are the basis of a precise and constructive approach.

Thus the mosaic gives rise to the project and the project to the mosaic. The house is entirely of wood and covered with a lozenge pattern in chiaroscuro, colour upon colour. The separated letters of a phrase, of a

particular calligraphy, are the only decorative element on the facade. The small opaque windows are in alabaster.

An awning, first imagined in a leopard-skin pattern, hangs under the house leaning against the wall of the church, combining the associations of Byzantine tapestries with a naturalistic effect.

With F Poggioli

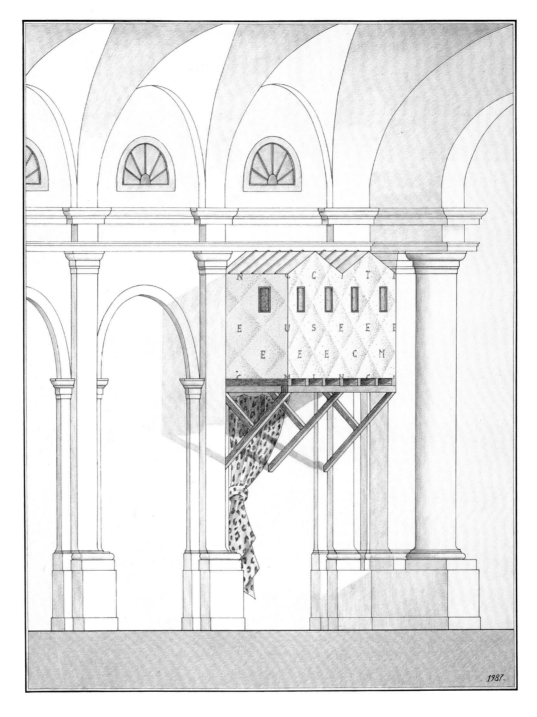

1987.

*OPPOSITE AND ABOVE: **View and perspective of house inside St Croce, Ravenna;** BELOW: **Sketches***

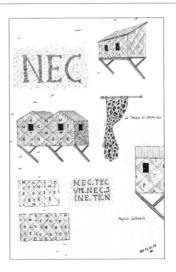

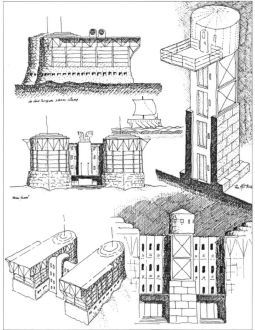

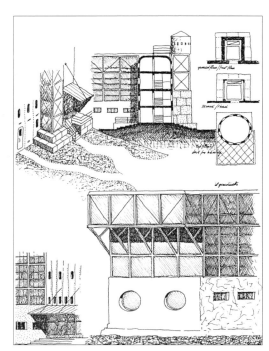

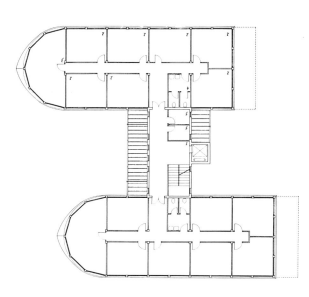

Brise - soleil in alluminio orientabili

Stuttura in ferro zincato a caldo

Infissi in alluminio anodizzato

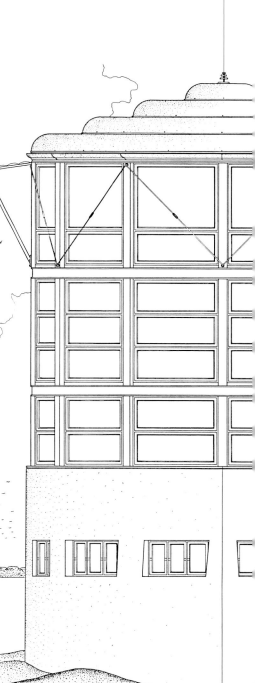

CLASSIS ACMAR OFFICE

RAVENNA, 1991

Minardi's determination to produce a noteworthy building for the head office of ACMAR, an important developer, was increased by its location in the outskirts of the city, an area often associated with haphazard planning and lack of quality.

He conceived this complex, adjoining the vaguely defined limits of the city, in terms of the prows of two ships. These look out across the countryside to the distant basilica of San Apollinare in Classe, standing as a memorial to that town's ancient Roman harbour. The

initial concept coincided with an idea for the ground plan in the form of an H. The lateral - 'sticks' rise four floors. The floors are independent of each other and can accommodate different configurations of rooms; they are joined by the cross bar which contains the entrances, access to the floors, and the services.

With G Grossi, S Polano, L Zaganelli

Intonaco inpastato con schegge di vetro

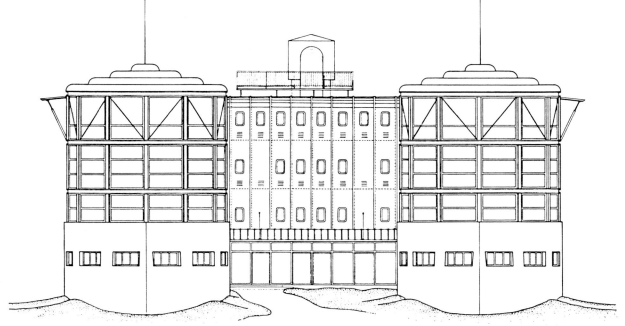

*OPPOSITE, FROM ABOVE
L TO R:* **Sketches;** *typological
plan; 6th-century mosaic
showing Classis Port,
Ravenna; detail of main
facade; FROM ABOVE:* **Model
views;** *elevation of main
facade; elevation of side facade*

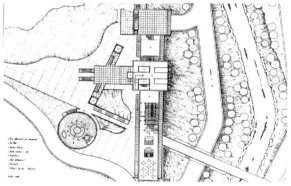

TOURIST CENTRE AND NEW FALORIA CABLEWAY

CORTINA D'AMPEZZO, 1989

This project was inspired by the tension produced by man-made structures in extreme natural environments: refuges high in the mountains, great cable-ways, and offshore platforms out at sea. The design consists of three parts: the hotel tower, the cafeteria built into the old bridge over the River Boite, and the cableway complex. The project is like a great machine in which the architectural components work together as in a gearbox, its most obvious element being the 'turbine' of the cableway station.

Everything is arranged to respond to the square's site in the mountains; this slopes down to the river, and is above a subterranean car park. The cableway complex is the main part of the project, housing the ski school office, rentals and workshop, a hang-gliding centre, a free-climbing centre, and a restaurant. The base of the new building is covered with the same rough-hewn stone as the adjacent bridge in order to impart architectural unity. Above the base the slender but powerful body of the building is covered with wooden panels,

a material which suggests mountain refuges. The windows are closely and rhythmically spaced, producing a perforated shell with views of the splendid valley scenery.

Degree project by Maurizio Lucca, supervised by Bruno Minardi, Venice University

FROM ABOVE, L TO R: **Perspective of north-west facade;** *ground level plan;* **Bonadé Bottino, tourist centre in Sestriere, 1950;** *OPPOSITE, FROM ABOVE:* **South-east facade; south-west facade**

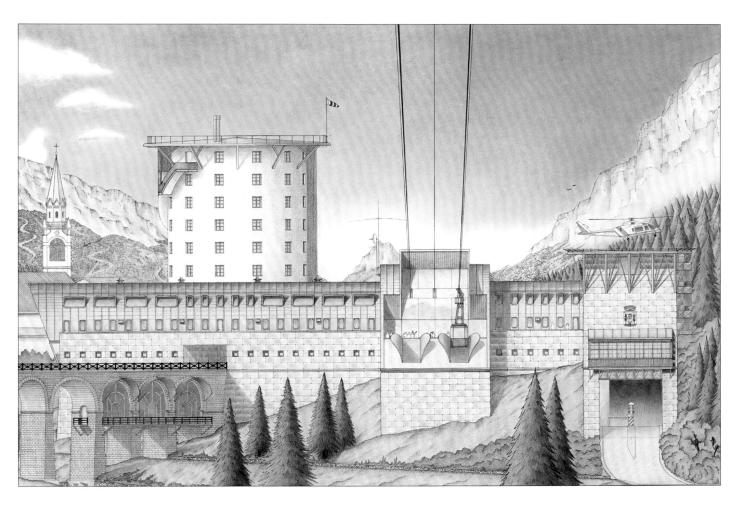

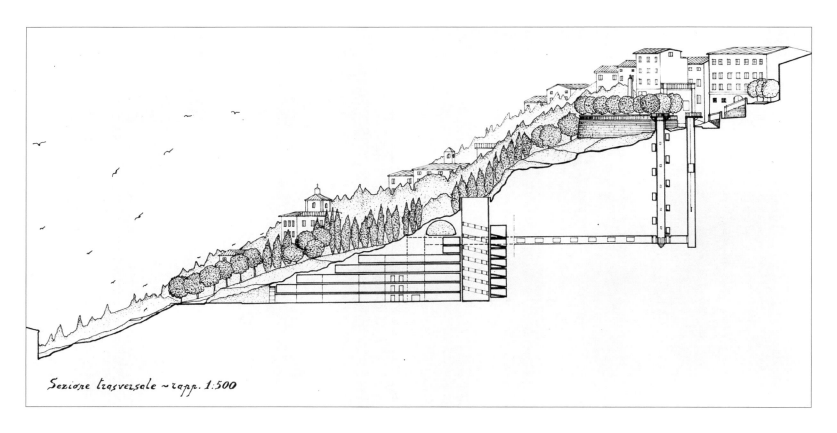

Sezione trasversale ~ rapp. 1:500

NEW TOWN GATE

CORTONA, 1992

This project proposes the construction of a large parking area to allow the centre of the Tuscan hill town of Cortona to become a pedestrian zone and to remove the need to park in the streets on the outskirts. The site lies at the end of Piazza Garibaldi, not far from the churches of Spirito Santo and Santa Maria delle Grazie al Calcinaio, where the provincial Cortona road enters the town centre. The car park is completely underground to keep vehicles out of sight and allow an unobstructed view of the countryside from the belvedere of the Piazza Garibaldi. Minardi's design also proposes a large pedestrian park connecting the square and the two nearby churches.

A tunnel, built in plastered cement, grooved to imitate stone, has a travelator to facilitate connection between the garage area and the square. A series of chambers line the tunnel enclosed behind reinforced glass; these contain reconstructions of Etruscan life: a kind of anthropological museum, and an introduction to the history and culture of the city.

Minardi saw that the vertical connection between the Etruscan tunnel – and thus also the garage – had potential. He thought of the tradition of wells – of that of St Patrick and also the ancient Roman well of Cortona. Here the vertical shaft is like a tower in which the outside becomes the inside of the well, and the inside of the stairs becomes the outside and winds around the earth. Like the entrance hall adjacent to Piazza Garibaldi, this is built in *pietra forte*, the local Tuscan stone.

With S Polano, L Zaganelli

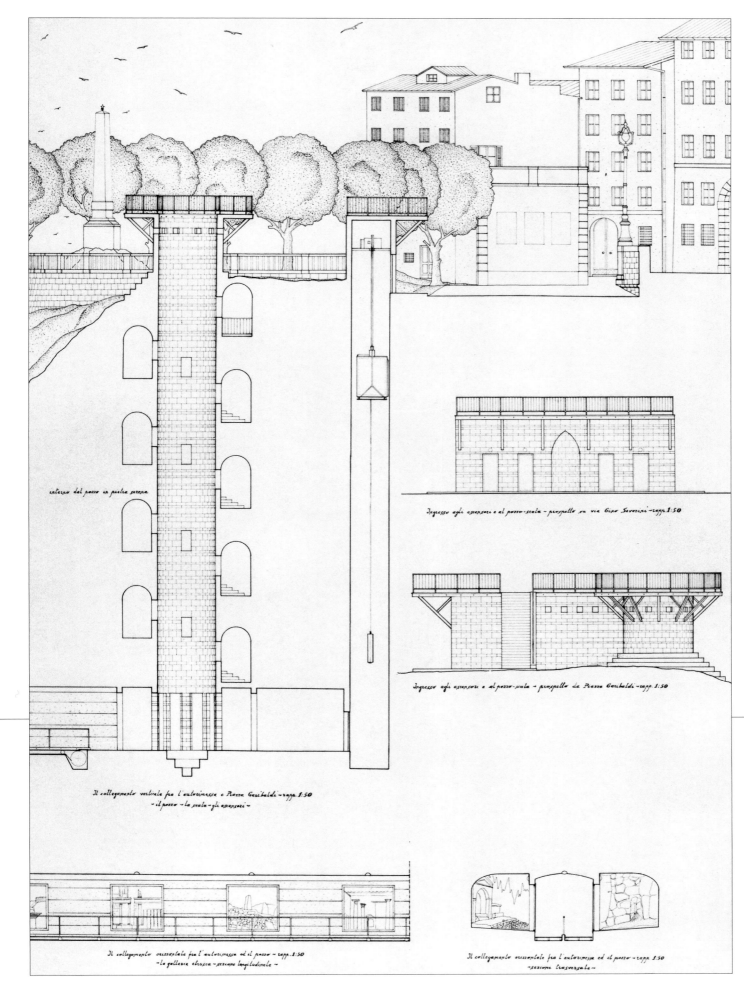

interno del pozzo in pietra serena

Il collegamento verticale fra l'autorimessa e Piazza Garibaldi – rapp. 1:50
– il pozzo – la scala – gli ascensori –

Ingresso agli ascensori e al pozzo-scala – prospetto su via Gino Severini – rapp. 1:50

Ingresso agli ascensori e al pozzo-scala – prospetto da Piazza Garibaldi – rapp. 1:50

Il collegamento orizzontale fra l'autorimessa ed il pozzo – rapp. 1:50
– la galleria chiusa – sezione longitudinale –

Il collegamento orizzontale fra l'autorimessa ed il pozzo – rapp. 1:50
– sezione trasversale –

OPPOSITE, FROM ABOVE
*L TO R: **Cross section; view of**
project site; medieval tower;
*THIS PAGE: **Cross section***
through well/stairs,
lift and gallery

'NOSTALGIA URBANA'

VENICE BIENNALE, 1990

Nostalgia Urbana is a large, 5-metre long acrylic painting executed by Minardi for the Venice Biennale with the help of his friend the painter Pino Pipoli. Here he collects together some of his favourite projects, combining them in a very personal landscape. The location is not a city and the building motifs, through which a river flows, rest on a background of familiar scenery. Between the houses and the hills there is an enormous field of wheat. Nostalgia goes hand in hand with melancholy and tender memories.

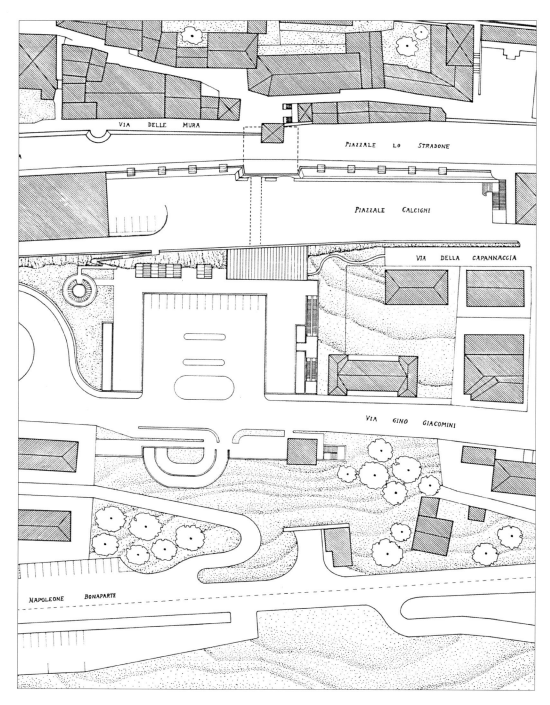

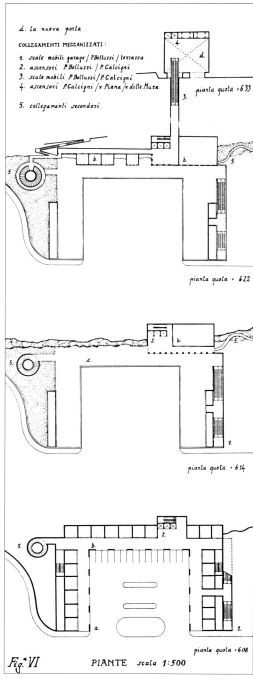

A NEW TOWN GATE

SAN MARINO, 1993

In the past municipal authorities undertook civic works of high quality to enhance the prestige of their cities.

Today this has become more difficult as urban populations lose their traditions and sense of place, a symptom of a more general decline in the urban environment and its social fabric.

The presence of motor vehicles has also had a detrimental effect on the ancient balance of the city, in some cases causing irreparable damage.

Minardi's new plan for San Marino, similar to that for Cortona, offers suggestions for solving the problem of access to the city. It does not attempt to remove traffic, but instead rationalises it in a way that reclaims and enhances parts of the urban complex which characterise San Marino.

As in Cortona, Minardi proposes some new buildings in iron, wood and glass, which he superimposes on the existing Belluzzi Square, the ancient walls, and the rock to overcome the current problem created by the different

levels of the old city and the new car park below. The new buildings, often dug into the mountain, connect the pedestrian ways with the help of lifts and escalators and blend into the medieval scene.

With L Zaganelli, M Gigante, S Polano

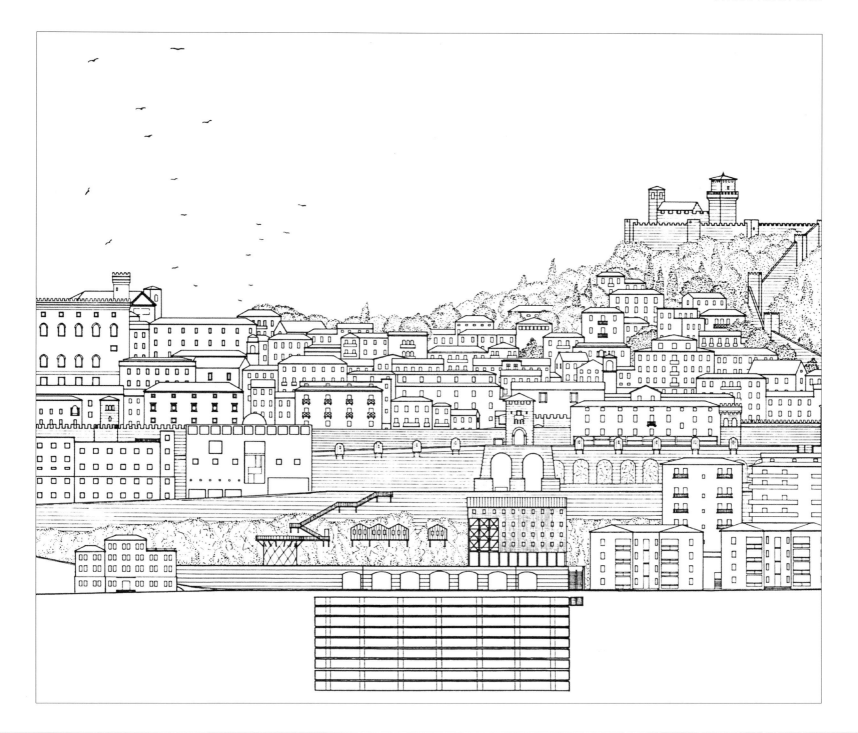

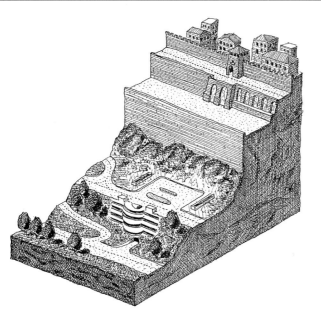

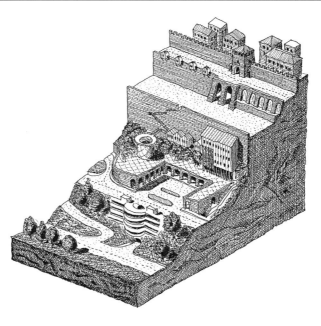

OPPOSITE, FROM L TO R: **Site plan; project plans;** FROM ABOVE: **Elevation of the town looking towards Montefeltro;** **isometric renderings showing the area as it is and with Minardi's project**

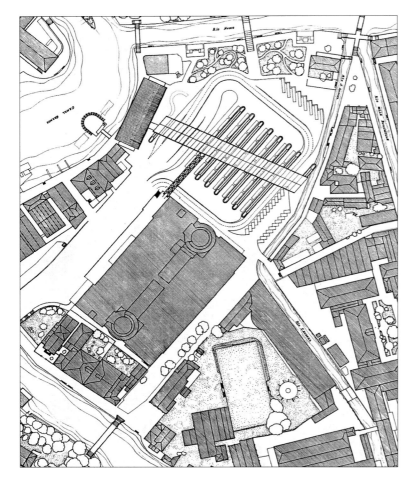
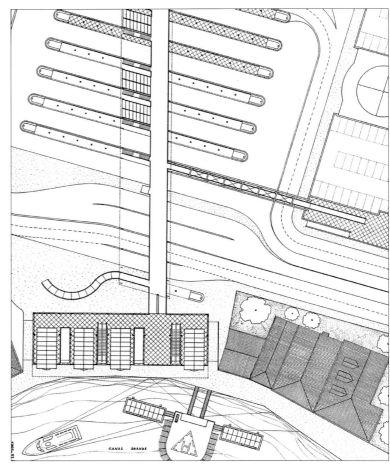

URBAN PLAN FOR THE END OF THE GRAND CANAL

VENICE, 1991-93

Minardi considers his creative process one of pondering images, of considering them in a physiological rather than an intellectual manner, of filtering and reassembling them into something new. Thus, his projects often exude a barely concealed nostalgia for the precepts and materials of a past age as well as a lucid awareness of their temporary nature.

His work, even when dealing with broad architectural themes, assumes a character which is fragmentary, split up and related to its surroundings; based on connection rather than

relationship. His is a technique of insertion: isolated architectonic elements find a *raison d'être* in calculated geometric relationships with pre-existing elements and their surroundings.

For this project in Venice, Minardi deals with vehicular access to the city through a network of roads, shelters and bridges which trace out a kind of flow chart on the asphalt. Means of access, stopping places and ramps are carefully rationalised in the proposed plan; the materials – the structural steelwork, the transparent roofs, the wooden planking, and

the stone used for the external, curved ends of the shelters – have been selected on the basis of what already exists in the area.

On one side of the square, in front of the houses that face it, is the San Andrea Canal which will be restored to use. On the other side, a building overlooking the Grand Canal will be converted to an embarkation point. This building hints at the structures of the Marghera industrial zone on the mainland, and is conceived as a typically Venetian port facility with its solid white base in Istrian stone

*OPPOSITE, FROM ABOVE
L TO R:* **Site plan; plan of
project; off-shore oil rig;
Antonio Canaletto, view of
the Grand Canal, 18th century,
detail;** *FROM ABOVE:* **Elements
of the project; bus station
elevation; Grand Canal
elevation**

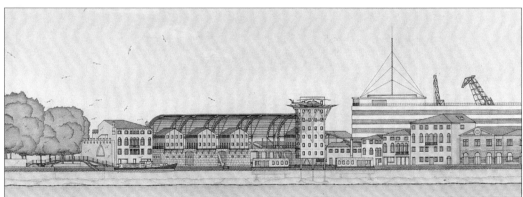

with various metallic fittings. Some mobile
steps lead to the top of the base, covered by
a large cantilevered roof lined with wood.
From here, the main covered passageway
leads to the shelters and garages in Piazzale
Roma. At this level, there are some metal
utility structures containing public services,
ticket offices, an air terminal, a bar and
restaurant, and everything necessary for an
open-air station on the waterfront.

With M Marega, S Serafini, L Zaganelli

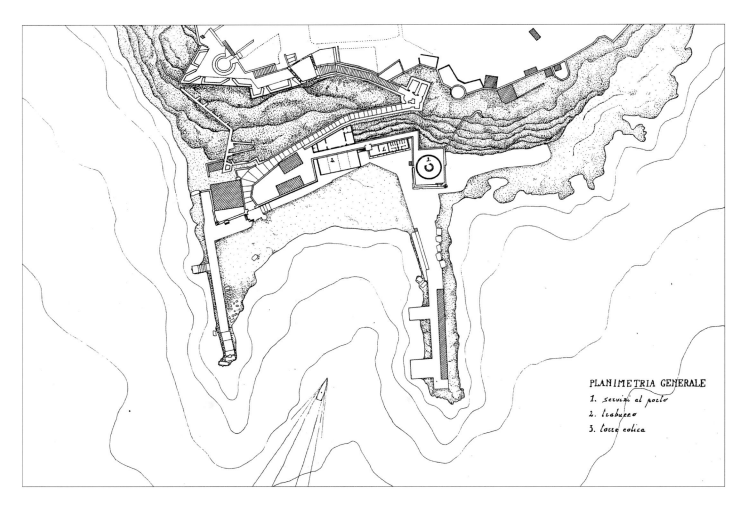

PLANIMETRIA GENERALE
1. servizi al porto
2. trabucco
3. torre eolica

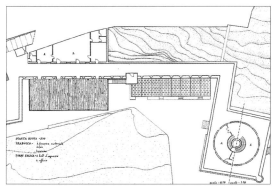

FROM ABOVE: **Site plan; first floor plan; second/third floor plan;** OPPOSITE, ABOVE: **Sketches;** BELOW: **Elevation and section of the wind tower**

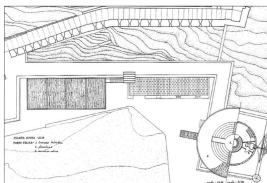

SAN NICOLA PORT

TREMITI ISLAND, 1993

Like the many layers of influence in his other projects, for the port of this island off the Adriatic coast of Italy, Minardi draws on a vocabulary rich in references and meanings. He cites 'the white Hanseatic window of Corunna (Spain); the fortress of Belém (Portugal), set in the water like a fossil shell; the profile of Tangiers, appearing as if by magic from the sea mist that melts on the ground; and Gibraltar, staring at Africa which looks back'. He draws on 'ruined pagan temples, small white churches, trees licked by the waves of the sea, lighthouses, large ships silent like ghosts, small harbours made of nothing, towers, castles, steep rocks sawn by blades of cobalt, and lazy beaches which anticipate slow plains'.

He is also aware of another way of looking at land, of seeing it not through the eyes of the land-locked but through the eyes of the sailor: the sea becomes territory bounded by land where its odours, colours, weather and climate are fixed to define countries and regions.

Many of these building types and features are present all around the Mediterranean in subtly varying forms: Saracen and Norman towers, windmills, lighthouses, water or diesel cisterns, small houses, precarious extensions hanging on to old stone structures. From these fragile elements, which over time have contributed to the definition of the Mediterranean as the home of classicism, Minardi conceived his ideas for this port.

His project is based on introducing some new buildings without altering the existing

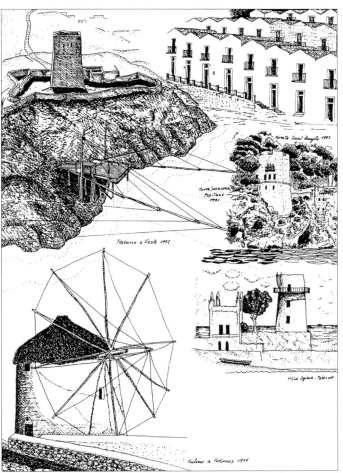

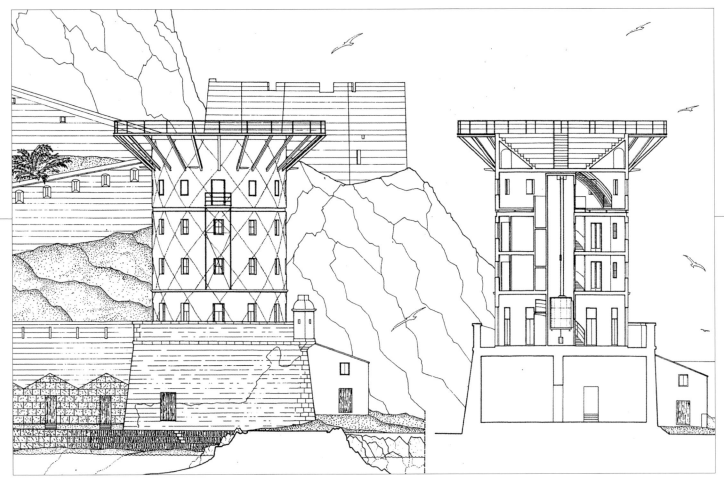

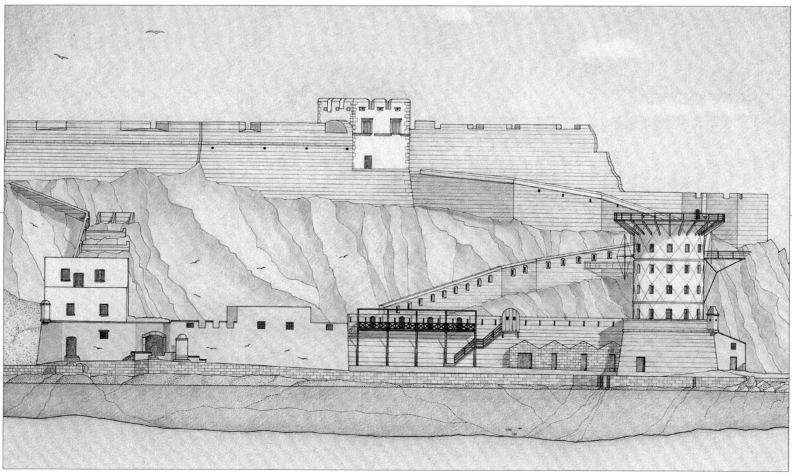

SEZIONE SCORCIATA

structures, while trying to enhance their use.
The main elements of the scheme are: the
stone houses, the Trabucco Restaurant, the
retractable ladder, and the wind tower.
Together they interact with the walls, the white
houses, and the keeps, to form a harbour that
is lastingly tied to its setting.

With L Zaganelli

OPPOSITE, FROM ABOVE: **Section through restaurant;**
principal elevation of port; FROM ABOVE: **Perspective; Nec**
Tecum Nec Sine Te, *pen and ink, 15 × 20cm*

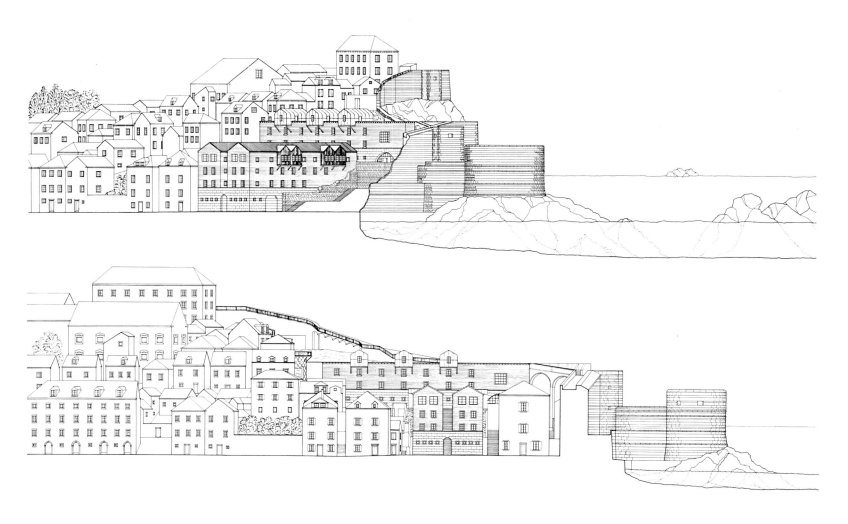

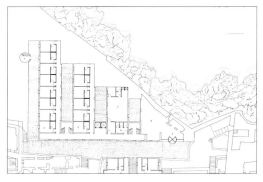
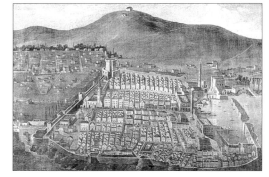
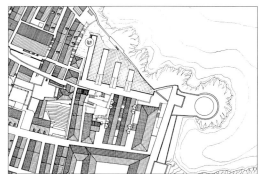

PROJECTS FOR THE OLD TOWN

DUBROVNIK, CROATIA, 1993

Prior to the Serb bombardment, Dubrovnik was one of the most beautiful cities in the Mediterranean. Built of Istrian stone, its compact and historic fabric was perfectly intact. These projects were produced at the start of the war, when damage to the city was limited, and offer suggestions for integrating some of the few pockets of the city which were still under discussion at that time. They stress continuity with the past but also a recognition of the present. They propose reconstructing two urban areas which were

vacant but in which there were signs of the past, the visible traces of old buildings becoming elements of the schemes.

The first plan is for a hotel in the western part of Dubrovnik in an area adjacent to the city walls; the second is for some residential buildings in the Pustijerna quarter, again near the city walls and close to the port.

Degree projects by Dionisio Fiocco, Paulo Manente; tutors: Bruno Minardi with Matteo Marega, Silvia Serafini, Lorenzo Zaganelli; Venice University

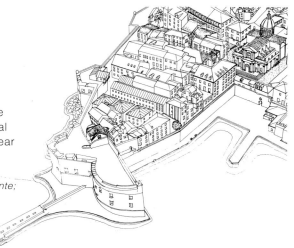

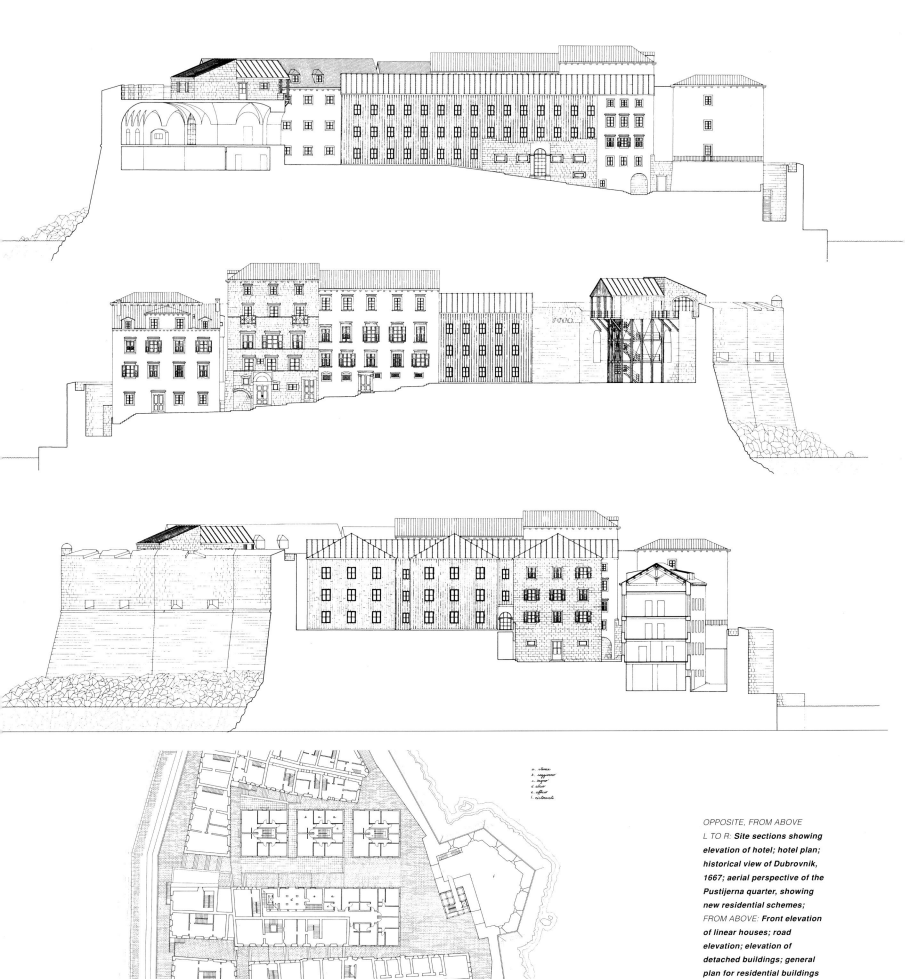

OPPOSITE, FROM ABOVE
L TO R: *Site sections showing
elevation of hotel; hotel plan;
historical view of Dubrovnik,
1667; aerial perspective of the
Pustijerna quarter, showing
new residential schemes;*
FROM ABOVE: *Front elevation
of linear houses; road
elevation; elevation of
detached buildings; general
plan for residential buildings*

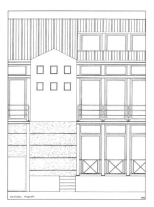
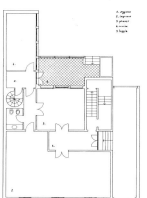

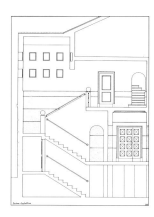

VITIELLO HOUSE

RAVENNA, 1991-93

This is an entirely remodelled house in the old centre of Ravenna. It is part of a larger complex which includes a building designed by Camillo Morigia at the end of the 1760s. The original house on the site had been completely reconstructed during the 1960s and was not considered of sufficient architectural value to be conserved. As part of his design process, Minardi studied the earlier architectural features, even though they were extremely modest.

The courtyard facade is conceived as an imposing stuccoed base with horizontal grooves creating a rustic backyard. Above this stands an iron and glass structure covering the facade and a compact tower which accommodates the stair. The house is L-shaped, which is typical of the terraced buildings in the old centre of Ravenna. Behind the frontal block on the street there is a projection rearwards on one side containing utility rooms; this defines a small courtyard. The L-shaped theme has not been lost through the addition in the corner of a veranda on the first floor and a terrace above

on the second floor. Inside the house the distribution of space is simple, according to traditional logic. Playing on the opposition of old and new, Minardi gives the interior an antique appearance. Particular stress is placed on the distribution of the principal spaces – the hall and stair – using a specially designed *trompe l'œil* imitating a covering of stone quoins and coffered ceilings.

With L Zaganelli

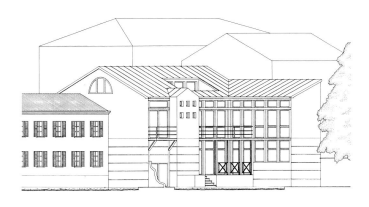

OPPOSITE, BELOW L TO R:
Courtyard facade; main staircase; mezzanine level plan; first floor plan; *LEFT:*
Perspective

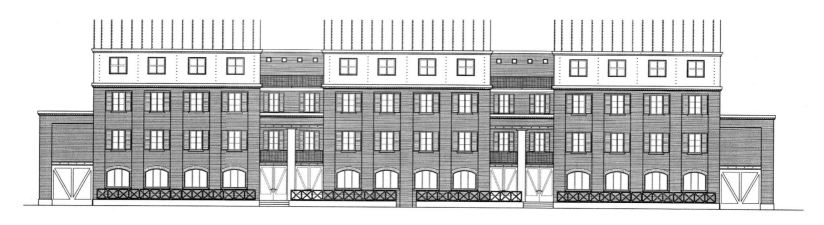

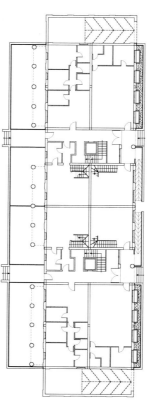

HOUSING IN THE FORMER POGGIALI SAWMILL

RAVENNA, 1992-95

The closure of the Poggiali sawmill and timber yard, which stands in the outskirts of Ravenna, offers an opportunity to recover an enormous area for urban redevelopment. The site includes a former slaughterhouse, a brick building with an inner courtyard, a beautiful nineteenth-century church, the apse of which is visible through the trees, and one other building, also brick, which once restored could accommodate shops and offices.

The proposed buildings, of which the largest is shown here, allow for urban spaces such as streets, small squares and gardens, while their architectural style reflects the facades and construction materials of the industrial heritage which gives the area its character and makes it a point of reference in the city.

With G Grossi, L Zaganelli, F Da Col

*FROM ABOVE, L TO R: **Elevation of main facade; model view; plan of mezzanine; model; 19th-century view;** OPPOSITE, FROM ABOVE: **Elevation of garden facade; model view; perspective view***

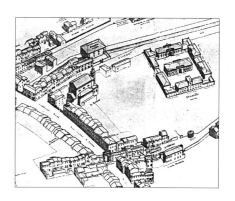

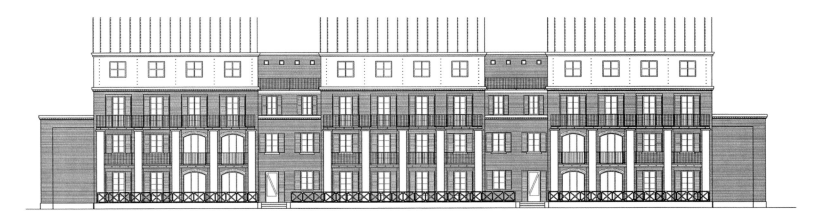

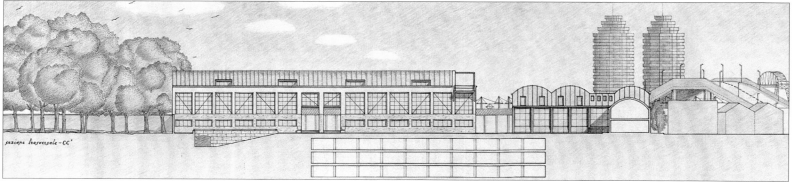

BUTON RENEWAL

VIALE MASINI, BOLOGNA, 1994

While the large Buton factory complex might be considered rather unremarkable, it has played a significant role in the recent history of Bologna's suburbs. Its closure and transfer to another site provides an opportunity to rebuild this large structure and return it to a more appropriate urban use.

The redevelopment includes offices, businesses and homes with a large underground car park to accommodate 300 cars.

The main building on Viale Masini is restructured; the others retain their shapes and volumes while undergoing extensive modifications to their facades, facing materials and roofs. The factory buildings are arranged around two squares, one paved, the other enclosing a large garden. In the area connecting these two squares there is a small cylindrical bar constructed in iron.

With L Zaganelli, Sahel Al-Hiyari, E Brunetti

*FROM ABOVE: **Elements of the project; section; site plan;** OPPOSITE: **Sections and elevations***

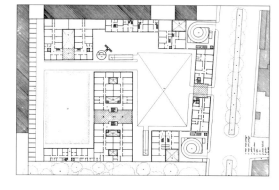

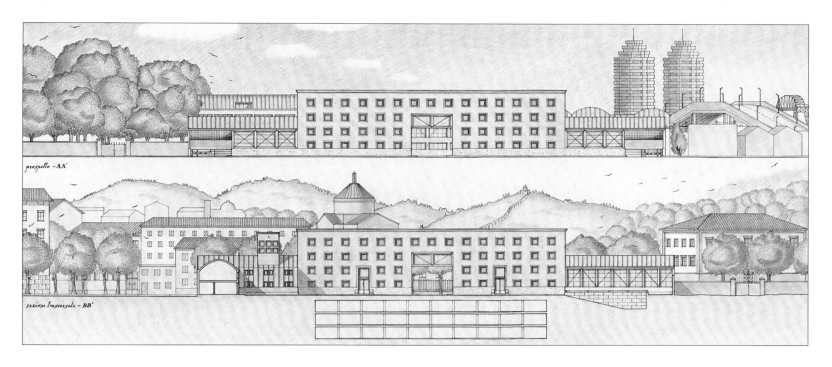

prospetto ~AA'

sezione trasversale ~BB'

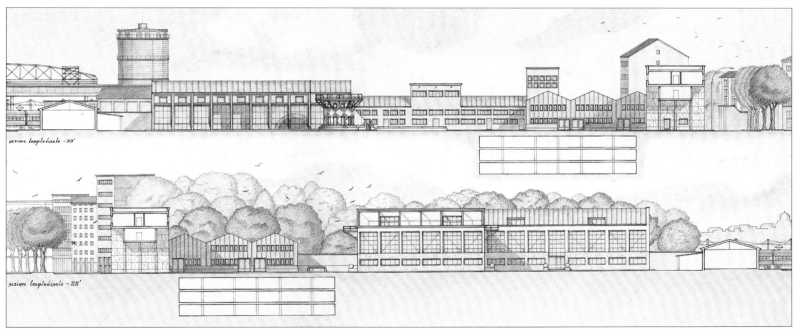

sezione longitudinale ~DD'

sezione longitudinale ~EE'

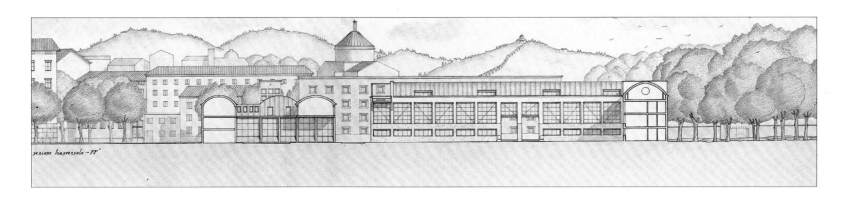

sezione trasversale ~FF'

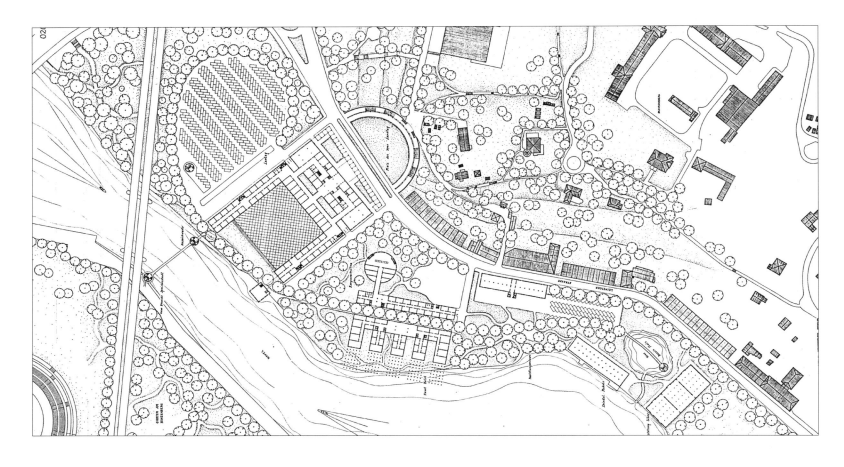

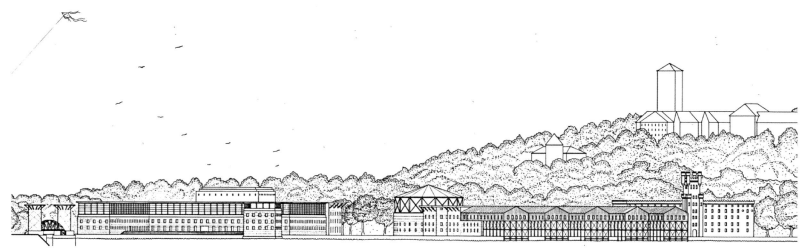

THE NEW SPEICHERSTADT

THE BRANDENBURG PARLIAMENT AND THE TRADE-FAIR CENTRE, POTSDAM, 1993

The southern bank of the River Havel – unlike the northern side with its large, carefully planned buildings – developed in a pragmatic, haphazard way producing a fragmentary layout lacking cohesion. This has resulted in a different kind of rapport with the water: the side of the old city seems to shy away from the river, whereas on that of the Speicherstadt the buildings come right up to the water's edge.

Minardi's design responds to these features. His parliament building required a programme able to combine diverse functions and forms

(a parliament hall, a library, offices, a restaurant, etc) and in order to achieve this, Minardi looked to similarly complex buildings in Potsdam – the traditional villas and castles.

On Leipzigerstrasse, opposite the portico and entrance to the parliament building, a great semicircular square opens out bordered by columns. On the other side of the parliament building, a very lightweight, narrow footbridge crosses the river in a single span suspended under an arched truss; this connects the city centre and the old Lustgarten with its public

buildings and the greenery of the Speicherstadt, forming a series of connected parks.

In front of the hotel complex, in a spacious green area opening on to Leipzigerstrasse, there is a cylindrical, multi-level building which contains offices, seminar and conference rooms – an arrangement affording flexibility in use. Behind this, the parallel wings of the hotel reach down to the river; they are built entirely in wood and are suspended from a double row of piles. A line of lime trees runs through the project area to connect the

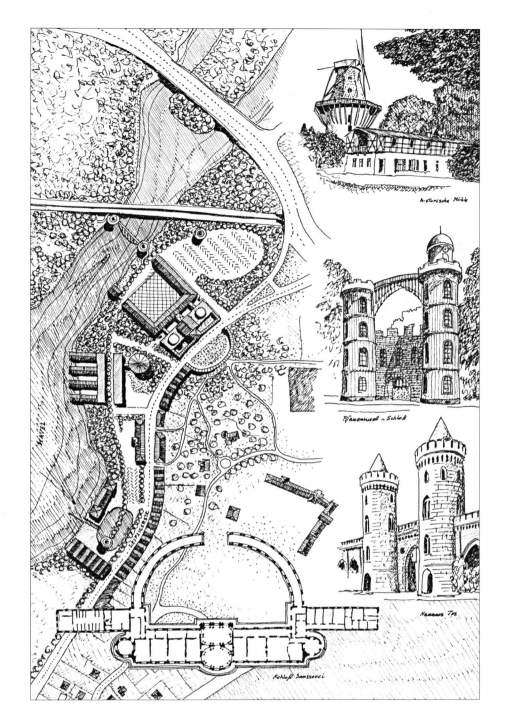

elements. The beginning and the end of this line are marked by two rotating observation towers from which it is possible to distinguish the more important monuments of Potsdam.

With S Polano, M Angelini, G Eliantonio, M Gigante

OPPOSITE, FROM ABOVE: **Site plan; view from the River Havel;** *ABOVE, L TO R:* **Sketches showing development of scheme and study of existing Potsdam buildings;** *RIGHT:* **Two 19th-century buildings, Sanssouci-Römische Bader, Potsdam**

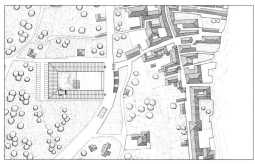
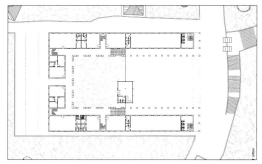
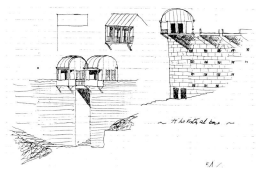

NEW PIAZZA DIANIA

ORTA SAN GIULIO, NOVARA, 1994

The nature of the locality and, in particular, its refined architecture were important considerations for this project. The layers of Piazza Diania seemed particularly suited to the construction of a large underground car park, to take advantage of the differences in level and the high circular containing wall. The car park has a capacity of 500 and is designed to be used by the residents, the inhabitants of the hinterland and tourists.

The project transforms the present square, freeing it from cars and affording it a court-like appearance open towards the lake. This arrangement forms a kind of gate way, a point of arrival for the city of Orta. The focal point of the square is a building with a plan similar to that of the convent on the island of San Giulio. This can accommodate a number of facilities such as banks, post and telegraph offices, a chemist's, and a tourist information centre in a way that makes access easy for non-residents coming from the surrounding suburbs.

The new Piazza Diania deliberately recalls the convent buildings with their courtyard. It is exactly this kind of building, often located in city outskirts, that stimulates the growth of suburbs around their decisive profile on the skyline. The aim of this project is similar: the new square will eventually mark the point of connection between the old city centre and the organic urban development of Orta.

Within this perimeter the square has two levels: the lower one paved and the higher one containing gardens. Where the two levels meet there is a small building which contains a bar – in its isolation this resembles the more

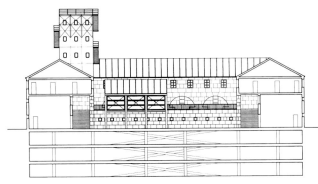 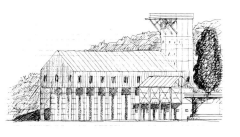 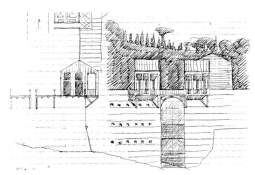

famous *broletto* of Piazza Motta. The whole is constructed in wood and stone, traditional materials of the area.

With S Serafini, P Bontempi, R Salmoiraghi, E Brunetti

OPPOSITE, FROM ABOVE L TO R: **Perspective; site plan; ground-floor plan; sketches;** *FROM ABOVE, L TO R:* **Cross section; sketches; cross section; Orta san Giulio from the lake**

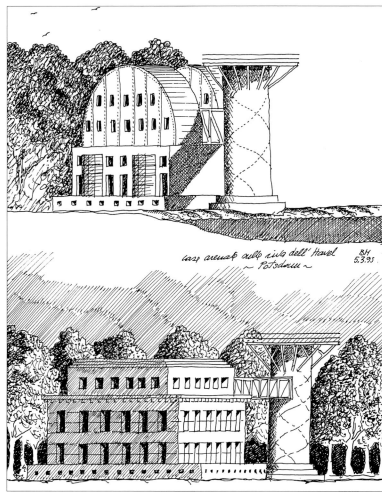

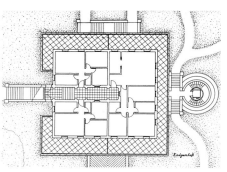

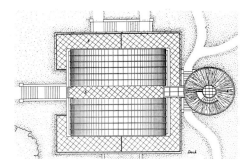

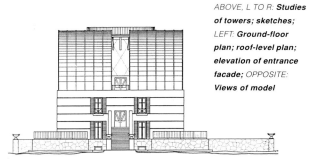

ABOVE, L TO R: **Studies of towers; sketches;** LEFT: **Ground-floor plan; roof-level plan; elevation of entrance facade;** OPPOSITE: **Views of model**

A NEW 'STADTVILLA'

BERLINER VORSTADT, POTSDAM, 1995

This project contributes to the planning of new residential neighbourhoods in Potsdam. In these areas, a new type of 'Stadtvilla' settlement is becoming common: this consists of isolated blocks containing apartments – town houses in the midst of green.

Minardi sought to fuse current building standards and techniques with the planning methods of Ludwig Persius, one of the most important architects of eighteenth-century Potsdam. In order to achieve this double objective, he analysed Persius' poetics,

identifying in his compositional techniques some modern methods ideal for reconstructing the desired complexity of the 'Stadtvilla' theme within a new and practicable project. He identified a formal repertory, the essential elements of which are the footings, block, tower with internal stairway, footbridge and belvedere. This could be developed into numerous variants.

Persius' work lies somewhere between a plan completely in agreement with the fundamentals of classicism and the world of

eclectic influence. Likewise, Minardi wanted to express a dialogue with other memories and so proposed complex analogies: with the North, for example, which he sees looking back to Classicism while dreaming of the Gothic fable – the sloping roofs of Dutch houses, Bruno Taut, Expressionism . . . From these he divined a metallic double mansard (which could also be in wood) which locates the project once and for all in the city.

With F Da Col, S Polano

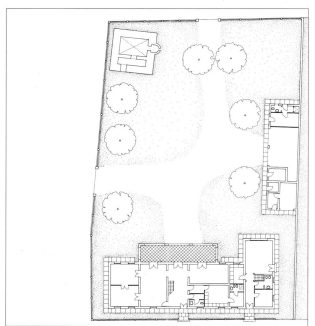

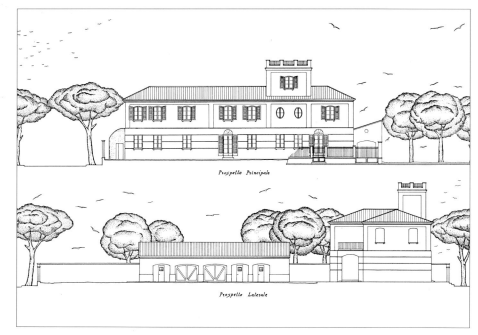

TROMBINI HOUSE

MARINA DI RAVENNA, 1994

The urban villa, understood as a one-family house with an independent garden, has contributed to the definition of the modern city's residential neighbourhoods. Entire areas have been progressively built up from it: Victorian London, for example. However, in recent times the lack of norms and rational points of reference has inevitably led to a loss of identity and confusion in city outskirts.

Minardi is convinced that regularity and repetition are important elements in any correct approach to the construction of the city. In the design of this villa he deliberately incorporates some elements from the urban villa genre, specifically that of the seaside resort; these include garden porticos, terraces, towers, the disposition of mass and also the use of materials, decor, finishings and colours. Minardi demonstrates that within this formal repertory, it is still possible to make choices and modifications, and to propose new solutions and variations.

With L Zaganelli, E Brunetti, M Rossi

FROM ABOVE, L TO R: **View from the garden; ground floor plan; front elevation; side elevation**

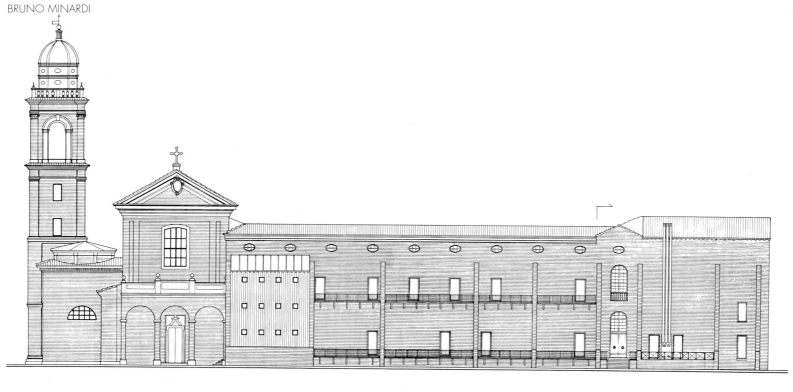

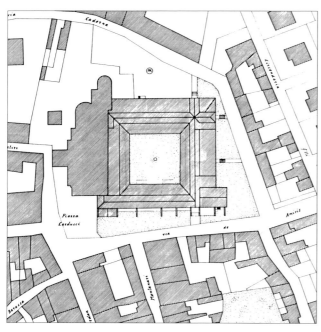

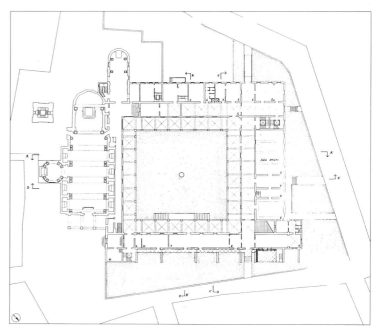

RESTORATION OF THE CONVENT OF SAN FRANCESCO

BAGNACAVALLO, 1995-96

At San Francesco Minardi had to address two issues: how to reuse a historic structure, and the cost of its conversion. Finding solutions to these problems is always more difficult in small towns or in areas away from main roads.

Here Minardi divides the convent into different types of space, to attract a variety of investors and to achieve a more measured relationship between the subdivisions of the enormous spaces available. The different kinds of facilities – which the investors have already requested – are part of a general plan in which the cloisters become the central connecting feature. The various kinds of premises can be reviewed at a later stage, and their user's requirements assessed as necessary.

Minardi's solution conserves the present form of the building, which is marked by successive restorations and a fragmentary architectural language. In this spirit, the structurally necessary addition of some buttresses to reinforce the facade along Via de Amicis aims to recall the memory of buildings, no longer existing, along the old supporting walls. Minardi adds a small structure built of dry materials, treated and oxidised to match the existing colour shades: wood-panel facing, iron framework for the stairs and lift, and lead sheet for the roof like that of the nearby bell tower which flanks the convent. In the wall of the facade the old doorways are re-opened as emergency exits, giving access to iron platforms which provide a visual link between the new buttresses.

With G Grossi with M Rossi, L Zaganelli

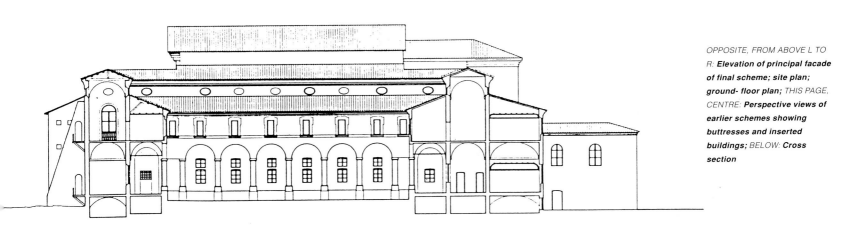

OPPOSITE, FROM ABOVE L TO R: **Elevation of principal facade of final scheme; site plan; ground- floor plan;** THIS PAGE, CENTRE: **Perspective views of earlier schemes showing buttresses and inserted buildings;** BELOW: **Cross section**

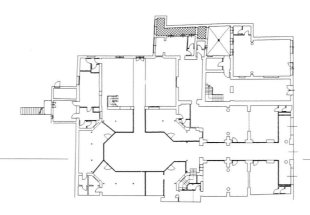
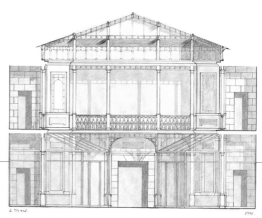

ANGELO FABBRI MALL

RAVENNA, 1996-97

At the beginning of the century, a draper's shop was built in the centre of Ravenna on the site of an old, open-air theatre; this large shop, covering 1,200 square metres, took its shape from the building it replaced. Constructed mainly in cast iron and glass, this structure is rapidly becoming one of the most interesting pieces of architecture in the city.

Today, for the inevitable economic reasons, this jewel of industrial archaeology is to be converted to accommodate ten shops and a cafe.

Minardi conceived this conversion as a new porticoed mall connecting the large hall with the outside, presenting a new facade to the street. The mall, with its new internal facade, houses shops and display windows, while the large hall, divided by glass set in an iron framework, accommodates individual shops. The corners of the large atrium and the staircase are decorated with stone *trompe l'œil,* and the air-conditioning pipes are incorporated into the interior decoration. The whole is lit by a large restored skylight and a new skylight above the entrance. This arrangement creates dialogues with the old building without imitating it. In order to enhance the innovative and elegant continuity between the old and new, all the metal structures are painted in the same ivory white.

With L Zaganelli, M Rossi, E Brunetti

*ABOVE, L TO R: **Ground-floor plan; section***

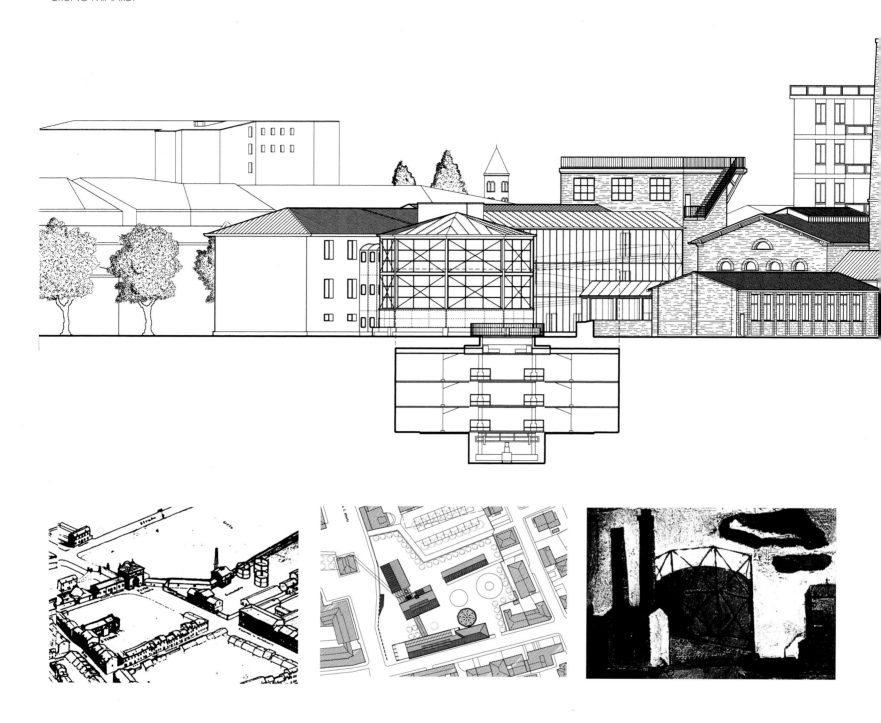

PUBLIC OFFICES IN THE FORMER GAS WORKS

RAVENNA, 1966

Minardi's scheme makes provision for offices, a canteen, a conference room and a car park, and reflects the varied urban fabric of the area. A few buildings on the site remain in their original late nineteenth-century form, others – such as the gas towers and a building on Via Roma – have been destroyed, while the office complex on Via Venezia incorporates a number of buildings within its structure.

The removal of part of the brick wall along Via Roma opens the front of the complex to the street, forming a triangular paved forecourt.

From here the main entrance leads to the offices and conference room. The entrance opens into a light-filled, iron and glass framed hall connecting two renovated brick buildings.

A glass passage connects this group to the smaller block on Via Venezia. Here a glass volume containing ramps and stairs is inserted to overcome the problems caused by the different floor levels of the existing buildings.

Two extensions were also necessary: one provides a facade on Via Roma – designed in salvaged bricks – and a second – built on the foundations of one of the former gas towers, and imitating its structure – accommodates new offices. A remodelled building in the courtyard houses the canteen, and a car park for 50 cars occupies the site of a second gas tower.

With C Sadich, L Marchetti, F Da Col, V Leoni, B Mariotti, S Trevisani, M Valeri

FROM ABOVE, L TO R: **Elevation from courtyard; Gaetano Savini, View of Ravenna, 1903; location plan; Mario Sironi, Paesaggio Urbano, 1943; perspective views**

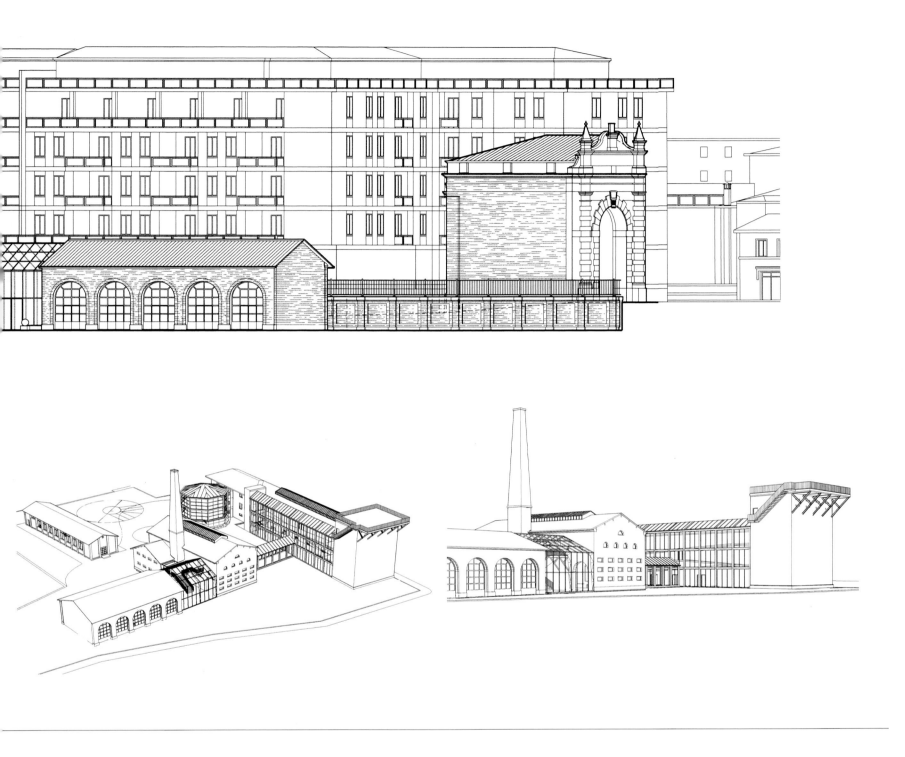

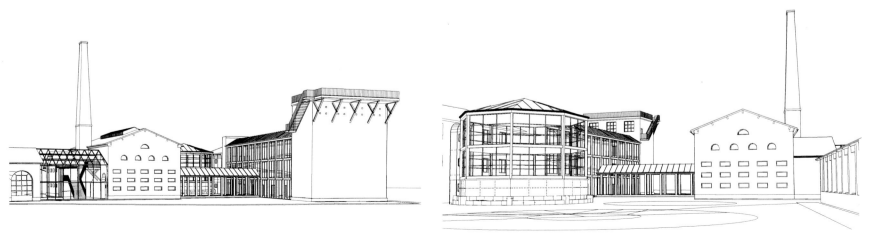

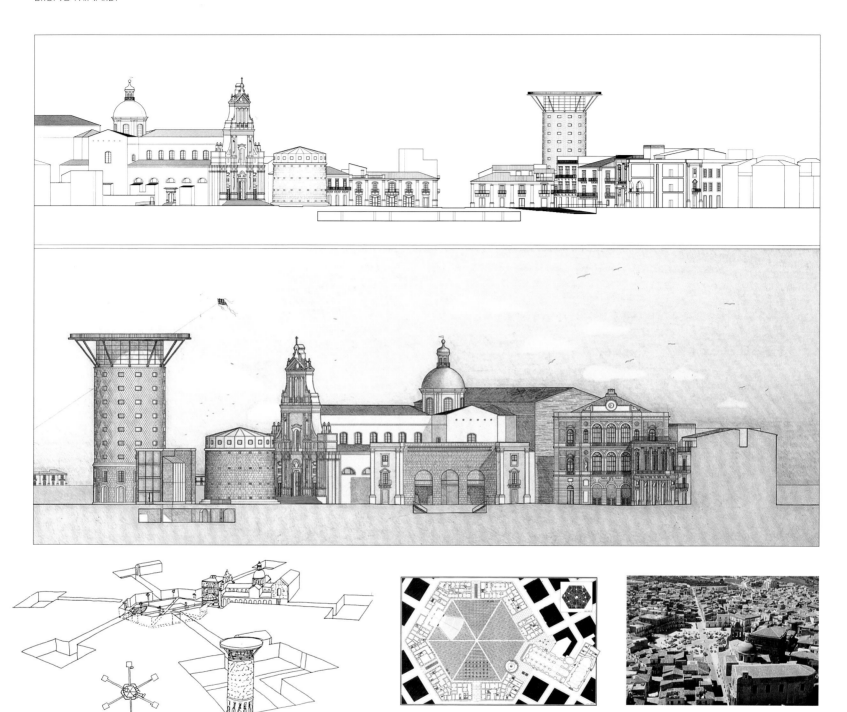

CARLO M CARAFA SQUARE

GRAMMICHELE, SICILY, 1996-97

Grammichele is a small eighteenth-century village in the heart of Sicily, built on a plan of concentric circles. Minardi's scheme is a competition entry for the improvement of the central square and is based on the introduction of certain architectonic elements such as a civic museum and arts centre, a theatre and local centre, and a hotel.

The museum is a large tufa stone tower with a copper-covered attic. It is located slightly off-line from the Corso Roma which creates space for a small square. An underground connection links the museum to a small building at the front of the square. This contains offices, services and meeting rooms. A blind wall closed in by a large glazed area houses the main archaeological exhibits.

The theatre is located on the square's other opening to the Corso Roma. It has an oval footprint, part of which is sunk into the ground. The half which rises – a two-storey, C-shaped building – is tufa stone in the centre, with two side wings in plaster. The windows and pilaster strips relate to those of the surrounding houses.

Minardi's plan includes a new hotel for the Piazza Dante, just outside the competition area. The cylindrical form of this is clad in majolica tiles typical of Sicilian architecture, while a glazed double attic opens towards the city.

With C Sadich, V Leoni, B Mariotti, S Trevisani, M Valeri

FROM ABOVE: **Elevations; sketch; site plan; village square viewed from the north-east;** *OPPOSITE, ABOVE:* **Computer renderings showing urban form;** *BELOW, L TO R:* **Sections, elevations and plans of museum; theatre; hotel; town plans**

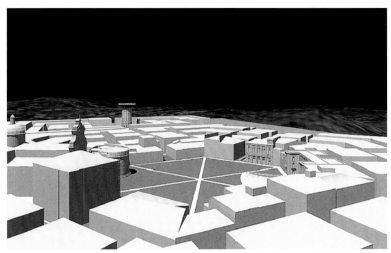

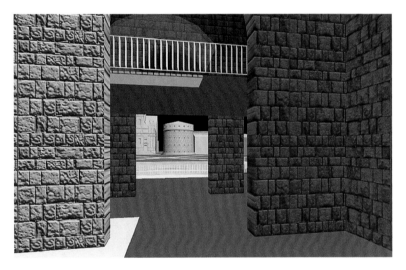

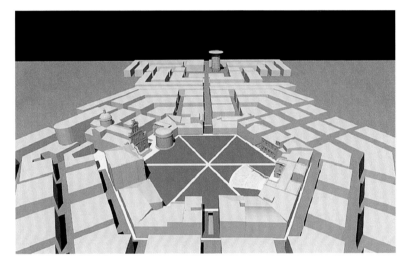

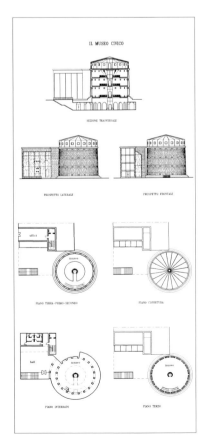

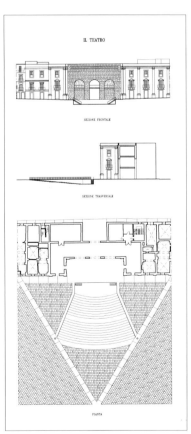

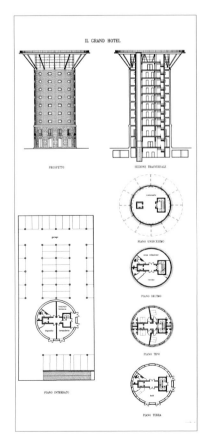

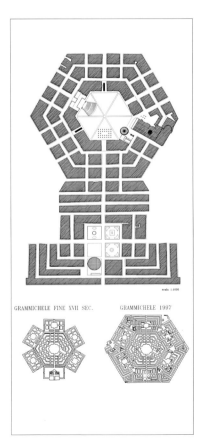

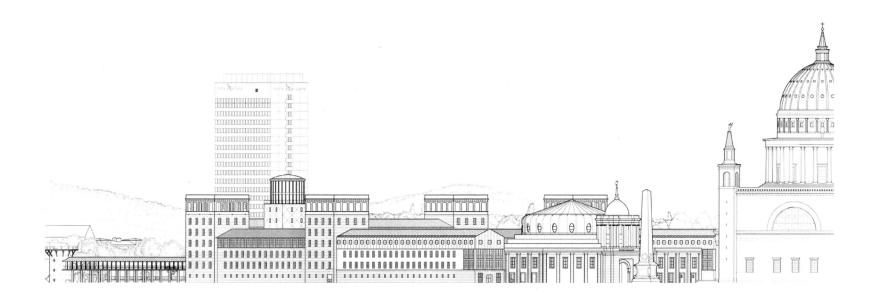

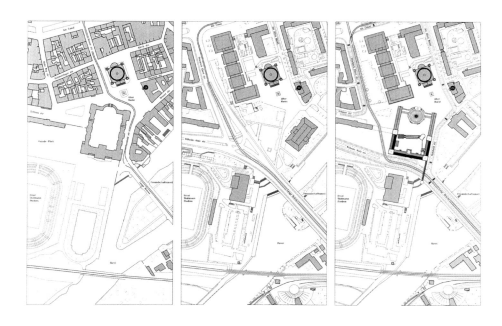 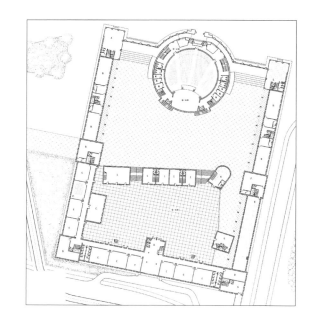

THE NEW STADTSCHLOSS

POTSDAM, 1996

In Potsdam, the 'Versailles of Prussia', the disappearance of the castle has left an empty space in the city centre. This scheme arises from the need to upgrade the area of the old marketplace and proposes another building which imitates and evokes the old Stadtschloss.

The various phases of the castle's growth are visible in the new building: from the ancient castrum with its watchtower – a kind of museum in the new version – right up to the 'Residenz Stadt' phase which offers three different aspects to the onlooker.

The castle's front elevation, which faces the Altes Markt, was conceived as an accurate reconstruction of the old gallery, the entrance gate of which is adapted to become a filter between the old square and the courtyard of the new building.

In order to generate an urban atmosphere, the scheme proposes a system of squares offset from each other: one for public use serving the round theatre, the shops and offices; another serving the university, the students' halls of residence, and the library.

The decision to allocate the squares mainly for public use was necessary in order to revitalise the area which was once the main city centre but has now become almost an outskirt.

Degree project by Valeria Leoni, Sonia Trevisani, Moris Valeri; tutors: Bruno Minardi and Silvia Serafini; Venice University

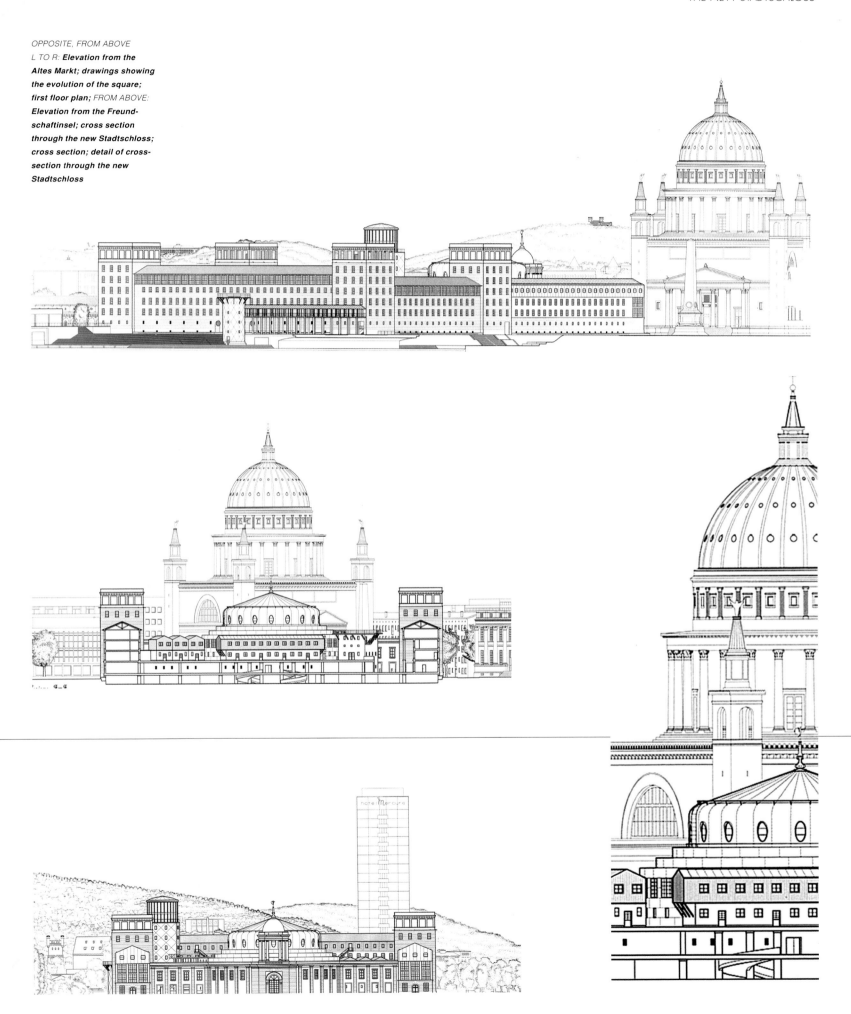

L TO R: **Elevation from the Altes Markt;** drawings showing the evolution of the square; **first floor plan;** FROM ABOVE: **Elevation from the Freundschaftinsel;** cross section through the new Stadtschloss; cross section; detail of cross-section through the new Stadtschloss